The Ocean Inside Me

A Spiritual Memoir on Healing Racial Trauma

R.G. Shore

ISBN: 979-8-9895219-0-6

Northwest Wisdom Publications

Book cover design by: Emily Mahon

Praise for THE OCEAN INSIDE ME

"In this searing, vivid first-person account, Mr. Shore recounts his journey – of abuse, oppression, healing, and love. Having been a prisoner of racism, the prison system, his own ignorance, he turns within to discover that his emotional and spiritual wounds turn out to be the portal to the love and compassion that heals. Love and justice, love over justice. A must read."
  – Mark Unno, Professor and Head of Religious Studies, University of Oregon

"A beautiful and heart-breaking tapestry woven from radios, racism, silence, and violence. A compelling invitation reminding us that true freedom must be pursued from within."
  – Philip Cox - Founder, The Inside Job

"This book takes you on an amazing and challenging journey to hold onto one's heart and soul as a person of color incarcerated. A powerful and heart-wrenching story of profound spirit."
  –Fr. Jim Galluzzo, Director of Diversity as Gift

"The Ocean Inside Me is partly a moving memoir and partly a guided meditation that helps readers connect to themselves in even the most chaotic circumstances...the author radiates a refreshingly compassionate way of seeing the world."
  –Indies Today

"R.G. Shore shares an incredible story of his incarceration and marginalization as an educated brown man in a White supremacist-dominated Oregon prison. Mr. Shore's writing vividly captures the contrast between the profundity of his inner experience with the harsh realities of his external environment. Somehow, these meditations begin to transform his understanding of himself, and a path begins to emerge leading him toward understanding his purpose and connection to humanity. We are fortunate to be guided by such a journey to explore our own capacities contained within."

–Alex Greene, Founder, Red Beard Somatic Therapy Internal Family Systems Practitioner

"*The Ocean Inside Me,* Mr. Shore shows us the power of meditation through the telling of his dramatic personal story. Woven through his compelling narrative are practices readers can use to explore and connect with the vast reaches of their whole being. He beautifully demonstrates the power of trusting the body to be a gateway to greater self-awareness and healing. As a white man dedicated to transforming my community into a more loving and inclusive space for all, I am also grateful to Mr. Shore for giving us a glimpse into the struggles of being a brown man living in predominantly white spaces. *The Ocean Inside Me* has led me further into the life-giving rewards of meditation and mindfulness."

– Tom McLaughlin, World Religions Instructor and Founder, Telios Projects

CONTENTS

Author Note

A note about the autobiographical nature of this book

I'm not sure where trauma takes us spiritually. Looking back at my time in prison, I think my meditations were protecting me from real danger and real trauma my body didn't otherwise know how to handle. I know my meditations were also leading me to a kind of healing that I couldn't find anywhere else. That is the truth.

This is my story; it is a story of real events and real experiences that took place within my body. This book is a spiritual memoir based upon my time incarcerated as a person of color in a very dangerous and racist place. This story is based upon my present recollection of past events – in particular, my experiences with meditation while in prison – what I learned and what I uncovered about myself. It's important to say that I waited a few years after being released from prison to begin writing my story. I knew I needed time to process and time to heal and sit with the wounds. Prison is not easy, and there are still many wounds to mend. This book contains content that is not always easy to hear or read about. Furthermore, this story is not a story that condones any crimes or any actions that cause hurt for others. On the contrary, this story is a story that only condones the transformation that can take place after the wound.

In being true to myself and to the events that took place, I did my best to recreate my story based upon conversations and meditations from my memories as they happened. I also used notes from personal journals and notebooks that I wrote in during my time in prison. My story contains personal judgments and opinions that reflected my own need for growth and self-awareness at the time. While this is a true story, names and characteristics have been changed in order to maintain anonymity and respect for other people and places a well.

A note about language

My story contains some language and content that may be graphic or triggering for readers. It is not my intention to glorify any form of hate as it may appear in the book. I do not support any form of discrimination, racism, violence, bigotry, sexism, homophobia, or hate of any kind. It is only my intention to give an accurate depiction of my experiences as a person of color in prison. Please note that you will at times encounter language that is racist, homophobic, sexist, and prejudicial.

I wrestled for quite some time with whether I should use the N-word, as well as other racial or homophobic slurs, in their full form. In the end, I felt like it was important to do so. I felt like it was necessary to accurately depict prison life as I experienced it. My story is about going inward and experiencing spirituality from within the body. My understanding of spirituality is that it has to involve sitting with the deeper wounds, allowing the hurt, and grieving the loss. I felt that it was important to write this book in a way that the reader could sit with me in my pain and in my own wound.

The truth is, we have the power to heal with our words,

and we have the power to hurt with our words, too. I will never condone these words, nor any other words that create wounds for others. We all hold trauma, and we all hold hurt within us. Often, we aren't aware of the harm that these words can cause. As I reflect on my own use of language, how I use my words, and how they affect others around me, I can only continue this journey of growth, self-awareness, and commitment to learning about my own biases and prejudices.

A note about spiritual story telling

I didn't write this book to avoid responsibility for my actions. I didn't write this book with an intention to spread any of my own trauma. I believe our bodies can carry real hurt and hurt has a real effect on others around us. In sharing my story, I am aware of the possibility that my personal trauma may be triggering, but it is not my intention. The purpose of my story telling is to promote healing and connection. In learning about my own wounds, I was able to learn about the wounds of others around me – often people that I didn't like. But this is the spiritual journey – to let go of our hurt in a way that helps us to carry the hurt of others.

Spirituality has taught me that the Universe is here in this moment, and we are a part of it. In being a part of this much larger existence, we are asked to hold and allow the harder things within us, too. The spiritual journey involves the shadow as much as it involves the light. When we are willing to go down deep into the shadows of our wound, we gain access to the deepest waters of our own heart. True story telling asks us to go there and learn to be gentle with ourselves.

A note on the Meditations

It is my intention to provide you with small how-to meditations at the end of several chapters so that, by the end of this book, you too will be able to drop into the visual meditations within your own body. You will be able to discover parts of yourself, buried within you, that have long waited to be found. I ask for your vulnerability and your trust as I humbly offer what I can. I cannot offer what I do not know but only what I have experienced.

Finally,

It's important for me to state that I am not a licensed therapist. Any content in this book regarding mental health and therapy is not professional opinion and should not be taken as professional advice. If you need mental health attention, I ask that you please seek a professional provider. While I am a certified spiritual counselor, I understand that each person is unique in their own experience. My opinions on spirituality are based upon my experiences in meditation. Please remember that, in the end, I am human too. I am learning just like you, making mistakes just like you, and growing just like you as well. Thank you for being gentle with me on this journey.

In kindness,
R.G. Shore

R.G. Shore

For Jess

"Here we sit with our souls tucked away in this marvelous luggage mostly insensible to the ways in which every spiritual practice begins with the body. Our bodies have shaped our views of the world just as our views of the world have shaped our bodies."

– Barbara Brown Taylor

PART I

Chapter One

Radio Static

I turn my radio up. There's a little dial on the side that changes the frequency. I slide my thumb up against the dial and, beneath the hissing sound of static, I make out a faint country song. But it's not what I want to listen to; I want the white noise. I slide the dial on the radio again until I hear the static come in like thunder. I have some old headphones plugged into my radio. I put my headphones over my shaggy hair, which I have tied up into a man bun. I put a navy-blue beanie over my headphones to help press the buds into my ears. Now, all I hear is white noise. I turn up the volume to the second dial, just below the first. I turn it all the way up, and a cool blast of static noise enters my eardrum. I am on my way inward.

My eyes are closed as I listen to the white noise growing louder. It's not jarring but soothing. The static begins to take shape, like a waterfall. Each wave of sound hits the base of my eardrum, thrumming itself into existence. I am standing in this waterfall made completely of noise. I am soaked in sound, but my skin is dry. I let the sound take me to where I need to go, deeper into thought, and deeper into my body, away from all these angry men.

The static from my radio drowns all the sounds out in the dorm. Their vulgarity and cacophony begin to mellow beneath the bursting radio static. Like falling on a slick patch of ice, the faces around me begin to blur; their details begin to thin. The racist thrum of chitchat fades quickly beneath the sound of my handheld radio. Before pulling my beanie completely over my eyes, I have one last thought: these aren't men, these are just boys in men's bodies.

無爲

I breathe in with the sound and I exhale with it too. Soon the waterfall of white noise morphs into rain pounding on the roof of some house. I am transported somewhere else within me. The scene is idyllic: a log cabin with a tin roof and smoke billowing from the chimney. I stand outside underneath the porch, listening to the pounding of rain against metal. I see the drops as they fall onto the metal above me. They are heavy, but each drop lulls me deeper into a primal rhythm created by some hum within me. My eyes are heavy, but I am awake. The pounding of rain on metal soon transforms into an ocean. Within moments, I am swallowed by a peaceful sea with its waves roaring above me.

I am faintly aware that this is still just a radio and that I am still here, wearing cheap headphones, lying on this bunk, which is not my bed. The static white noise coming through my headphones is now an ocean of waves crashing on large rocks, and I am looking up at them from underneath the water. It's loud above me but calm where I am. I can breathe under this water — this is not a nightmare of me drowning: this is a meditation.

I have found that meditation guides me into an unknown that I'd normally not go into. It leads me to the parts of my body that need discovering. But self-discovery is not an excuse to separate myself from all the people who don't look like me, or think like me; self-discovery, in fact, is the only thing that'll lead me to understand those people on a much deeper level. By going into the wounds of myself, I enter a much deeper pain that holds all other wounds.

Everything is weightless and dark blue down here. Everything is at peace. My limbs float loosely with the water. I hear the breath within my body tell me to become the ocean, to go deeper. So, I do. I start to sink into myself, in a tunneling-out kind of way, like a miner trapped in coal, but I'm digging to the center of this mountain — it's the only true way out.

The white noise from my radio continues to grow, undulating in my ears like calm waves on an ocean. My breaths are long now, maybe minutes. As I inhale, I hear the sound of my breath coming into my body. My inhale begins to amalgamate with the static playing through my headphones. I can feel my breath alkalizing now, the oxygen levels in my brain continuing to rise.

I envision an energy moving upward from the base of my spine with my breath. The energy rises from my Muladhara, or root chakra, up into the frontal lobe of my brain. I squeeze tightly, and the energy bursts into my pineal gland. My vision begins to fill my body with a warmth unfamiliar to this institution. The light within me grows brighter, and I start to make out an image, almost as if I'm peering into my memory, but it's not a memory at all. It feels like it's happening in real time. The scene is blurry around the edges but clear at the center, like a fish-eye lens.

Suddenly, I see my thirteen-year-old self sitting at a table in the school cafeteria with my friends. Though surrounded, he's completely alone. He's making them all laugh. He does a good job at that; he's a lifelong entertainer. He's funny and his eyes are large. His middle-school body — gangly and unearthed — matches his humor. His Brown skin looks odd in a sea of White. He has the body of a boy born in the southeastern part of the world, but his thoughts and his views are formed by that of the West. He uses his own awkward body to drive the butt of the joke home. His friends laugh, but he's still lonely. You can see it on his face, and he doesn't want anyone to notice it.

All of a sudden, my thirteen-year-old self sees me. This is not A Christmas Carol. He can see me, and he knows I'm watching him. He stares at me for some time before he says the strangest thing: "Who are you?"

He doesn't recognize me. I'm him, but seventeen years older, and still, he has no idea who I am. Is he really asking who I am? Why doesn't he know me?

Suddenly, I hear the ocean again, the sound of the white noise from my handheld radio growing louder. Then there is a whisper, a very gentle whisper amidst the burgeoning static.

I hear the voice pronounce clearly: Wu Wei.

This prison is packed full. You couldn't fit another pickle in this jar if you wanted to. Bunks are less than two feet apart. There's no space and certainly no privacy. Because there's no physical room in here, there's no room for emotion either. The men can't cry because there's nowhere to go. At night, men pull their beanies over their eyes. I imagine that's when they cry. I can't cry in here because there's no space to cry. Instead, I just pull my beanie over my eyes because it helps me move inward. When I cover my eyes, I can pretend like I'm not here. I know that I am, but it helps me to get where I need to go, which is out of my thoughts and into my body.

It's always so loud and busy in here. My radio and meditation save me from the murder of noise above me. I'm in a prison of five hundred very angry, very misunderstood men. Most of them look like bears without fur, peppered with stick-and-poke tattoos of swastikas, racist jargon, and malappropriated American flags (which often only have thirteen stars). Many of the men here have holes in their arms and holes in their teeth — blackened from extreme meth use. And the teeth that they do have are crooked, yellow, and jagged, and smell of tar and tobacco. Physique can be a paradox in here: men spend hours on the yard getting swole, only to go back to their bunks to veg out on soups (Ramen) and junk food. There's no blaming them, though, because prison food is shit.

There's a sweatiness about the men in here too. Their facial hair is often unkempt and greasy, and their voices are often flustered. Years of trauma and abuse have caused many of the men in here to feel paranoid and victimized. It's always everybody else's fault and never their own. I think there's a sweatiness that comes with being defensive.

The men who have been down (in prison) the longest are often overweight and stale. Inmates call them dump trucks. They remind me of seals on the coast that lie in the sun on the docks. These kinds of men don't have to go anywhere to make their moves. They have the younger ones come to them. They've been down so long they no longer care if they spill Cheeto crumbs on their beds because they know, every Monday, they'll get new sheets. Some of the old-timers are too lazy to get up at all; I watch them wipe the cheese from their fingers on their pillowcases — snacks for later, maybe? It's not a judgment but an observation. Prison teaches men to not care — certainly not about others but also not about themselves either. It's fast-food living. You don't shit where you eat, unless it's prison, because everywhere is shit.

I feel like I'm "a million days and a wake-up to the gate," which is prison jargon for how much time I have left before I'm free. It feels like I have an infinite amount of time to find out why I'm so wounded and to discover the healing I've long yearned for. The thing is, people on the outside don't want people like us to heal — that's why they put us in here in the first place. We are outta-sight-outta-mind kind of people. The thing about prison is it's a place that can quickly destroy you — mentally, emotionally, physically, and spiritually. Prison can also lead you to a healing that even free men don't often find, but you've got to be willing to do the work, which is the hardest part. And it's damn near impossible to try to heal the trauma when you're living in a place that serves it up twice as fast. Healing trauma in prison is like a recovering alcoholic trying to get sober at Oktoberfest, but it doesn't mean I shouldn't try.

Besides sleep, my radio is the only escape I get from the men around me. It's their snoring that reminds me they're human; I guess even White supremacists need to sleep. The dorm constantly smells of anger and fear. I can taste it in my mouth. Things are always tense. This place feels like a stadium full of fans who have just lost a home game. There's nowhere to go in here. I am stuck on this bunk. I can't go outward, so I have learned to go inward — into my body, into my skin, into my muscles. My breath, and the static from my radio, guide me here.

The words are clear, even through all the static and radio waves:

Wu Wei.

What is it?

I know I've heard that term before. I can't place it. But I know I've heard it. I'm not ready to leave this meditation yet. It's too important. Besides, what's waiting for me at the surface is far more destructive than what's down here. I want to stay down here, down in this safe ocean. I want to go back into myself and visit my thirteen-year-old self and ask him more questions, but I can feel myself starting to float back up into the prison. I can feel my thoughts tearing me away from the meditation. I'm now focused on the voice and not the inner stillness of the ocean around me.

Wu Wei.

What does it mean? Where have I heard that term before?

Breathing usually settles the busyness of my thoughts, but not this time. Instead, I find myself racing through my mind, fiddling through each memory like a thumb through an index file trying to figure out where I've heard the term before. Wu Wei. Is it from Merton? Is it from Zhuangzi? Buddhism? Daoism? I earned my bachelor's degree in religious studies, so my mind naturally goes there — to all the books I've read, all the terms I spent thousands of hours memorizing.

I rapidly list authors — Thomas Merton, D.T Suzuki, and Thich Naht Hanh — but there are so many terms and so many names, and now I feel flustered. I just want to stay down here in this meditation, but I can't. My restless thoughts won't let me. My body and mind are at war with each other, and my body is rapidly losing. My mind won't let go of the question:

What is Wu Wei?

I can feel my hands begin to shift. Tempted by my mind to throw in the towel, I feel my hands reach up to pull my headphones off and admit defeat, but suddenly the answer comes to me like lightning. I am not sure how, but it comes surging in just at the right time, washing over me like tidal waves of energy:

Wu Wei: non-doing.

I remember now. The name comes sizzling in my brain like bacon in a hot pan: Lao Tzu, the founder of Taoism. Lao Tzu, the legendary author to whom the writings of Tao Te Ching are attributed.

Wu Wei is a term that might be easily misinterpreted as "do nothing," but it's actually more about non-doing. Wu Wei isn't permission from Lao Tzu not to act; it isn't an excuse to be lazy. (Formidably, an excuse that many Americans would love to have.) I remember in college my professor explaining Wu Wei to the lecture hall. I remember some frat-looking guy shouting out from atop the auditorium, "Do nothing? Does that mean I don't have to write my research paper?" And I remember my professor's response, "Wu Wei, man…. it means…. you weren't going to write it anyway… Bro," to which the class laughed.

Wu Wei: non-doing. I remember now… but why here?

Why the subtle whisper deep down in the ocean of my meditation?

無爲

It doesn't matter, though, because now that I've recalled the term, my brain can relax. I sink beneath the water again. I can be at peace. My body has won. I feel the muscles in my jaw loosen. I take a deep, meditative breath, and I'm back beneath the waves.

I set my intention. This time it's simple: Just be here, just be here and listen. Listen to this ocean, listen to what it has to tell you.

And so, I sit.

What feels like hours down here is merely minutes up there, but that's okay because I like it down here. So, I take my own advice, and I listen.

This is what the ocean says to me:

Wu Wei is not about doing, but it's not about not-doing either. It's about noticing what is. You cannot see what doing is, or what non-doing is, if you aren't first noticing.

Notice everything, even if it's painful.

Prison is a place that can take the "noticing" away from you. It is a place that is all mind and no body, but your body is where the healing takes place. You can't force healing. It doesn't matter how strong you think your mind is; you must be willing to forfeit trying and move into letting go.

It is really about allowing and not forcing something to happen. Wu Wei is entering into a river and swimming with the current, not against it. It's funny: our whole lives we enter the river and face the wrong direction. No wonder our bodies are so exhausted and beat up by the end of things. We get in the water, and we look upriver. What if we were to turn around? What if we were to let go of trying to swim against the current, and instead, just flow with it? The doing can only happen through the subtle art of allowing it to be done to us. The doing only happens when we let go of trying to "do it" our own way. When we swim with the water, we become a part of it. This is Wu Wei.

Growing up, I did a lot of art. I was always a good artist, but the times I was a great artist were in the moments when I allowed the art to guide me, when I allowed the art to use my hand to put to paper what had always been there. Wu Wei is us participating with the Universe at this essential level. It is a "tapping into" and a "becoming" without the use of force, without the use of trying. Regardless of outcome, we are called to participate in this kind of allowing.

This Universal energy is the natural way of things, I think. Wu Wei is the Universe's default setting, but we often forget and try to create our own path forward. The Universe speaks a different kind of language than we do. It's not that the Universe has stopped speaking to us. Rather, it is we who have stopped listening to her. We've reached a point in time where most of us have forgotten her language entirely. We've forgotten what she sounds like, and we've forgotten how to interpret the signs that have always been there. When we stop and still ourselves, just for a moment, we can hear the faint language again — like hearing a song softly sung through a wall. Wu Wei reminds us to listen to the gentle melody. In art, the entire canvas is important, both the positive and negative spaces. In Wu Wei, both the positive and negative space in our lives are equally important.

In prison, however, it feels like there is only negative space. There are no trees inside the fence of the prison, only outside. There is very little access to the earth here. The men have been gathered like chickens in a coop, our feathers constantly prodded and poked by the harshness of our reality. No, prison is not an easy place to come to terms with Wu Wei because it requires us to be present to ourselves in a place where nobody wants to be present to anything. It requires us to be present to what is. Even though I am not a fan of what is — certainly not in this place — I know this current "isness" is where I am right now, so I have to try.

That is what meditation can do to you though. It can take you all the way in and then tell you to be still and listen. In meditation, you learn to create a safe space for yourself, and while prison is never safe, you learn to work with what you've got. When I started listening to the white noise of the radio, the first thought I had was, "This sounds like water." So that was the safe space I created for myself. The space is always available, you just need to be willing to create it first and then go to it often. The water is not the space itself, but a tool to get me where I need to go. You must feel safe: that is key. And you must be able to return to that same place.

無爲

The voice makes me wonder what I've been pushing for. When I first came to prison, I could feel the resistance in me. I could feel a force within me that wanted to push against the reality of what was. I was a man looking upriver. I wanted any kind of control over my life, and I didn't have it. I felt myself constantly pushing against what was happening to me, instead of allowing it to just happen. I was looking for an outcome that didn't exist. Men in prison constantly look for outcomes that just don't exist. It's all pain, but meditation teaches me that we're supposed to let the pain happen too.

I remember when I first came to prison, I was so scared and lonely that I just wanted some kind of connection, any kind of connection. It didn't take long to realize that connection with wolves is no kind of connection at all. It's true there is no honor among thieves and you are the company you keep. So, I learned not to keep any kind of company.

I learned quickly there's no real kindness in here. I learned that if someone is trying to be kind to you, it means they want something. In prison, kindness equals debt, and the interest on that debt is steep. One of the first tips I got in prison was to never owe anyone anything. So, I learned to be lonely with myself, which can often feel more painful.

I couldn't find connection with anyone or anything. I felt like that same kid in the cafeteria. I remember trying to get people to write to me. I had a friend sign me up for a pen pal site online, but I never got a single letter. No matter what I did, I kept pushing up against what was. There seemed to be no luck getting through to the Universe. Then my meditations began to subtly remind me to let go of what wasn't working and open myself up to the spaciousness of what was working.

無爲

Now, that spiritual voice comes in like a soft rain. Wu Wei reminds me that I can only hear this voice when I quiet myself and create a space to listen. Still, how am I supposed to create space to be still in a place like this?

I can feel myself moving around in this ocean. I'm

looking for a way into the peace, but I can't seem to find it. The white noise can only help so much. I begin to hear faint voices, but they aren't angelic and they aren't coming from down in this sea. They are coming from up above in the prison.

I can hear two of the inmates arguing by my bunk. One of them owes the other money.

"You said Monday, bitch. It's Monday."

"The fuck you just say?"

They are inches from my face. Though my eyes are closed, I can see their anger. It rises off their skin like heat waves.

No matter what I do, I can never get away. Why won't they just leave me alone? Why can't I get a minute of silence?

I can feel my restlessness poking at me from within. I can feel the anger wafting back in. I turn the volume dial up on the radio, but it's already as far up as it can go. There's a sense of panic, and I can feel the old patterns within me come to life. I want to throw my radio. I want to tear my headphones from my ears and blame the White God in the sky that probably doesn't exist. I try to picture the river — that river of stillness. These thoughts and patterns are a version of me looking upriver. What if I turn around and just go with the water instead? What if there was a way to invite the space?

Then the old thought pattern comes creeping back in:

Why am I constantly surrounded by the busyness of this shit?

These men can't ever just sit still with their thoughts, and men who can't sit still cause unrest for everybody else. There's no point.

Besides, I'm just one small Brown body in here. What can I do? My body is already working overtime trying to protect me, to keep me safe.

To say there is no space would be an understatement. To say there is opportunity for a person like me to create space in a place like this is an absurdity.

But then... I hear the voice again:

Wu Wei.

I pause and inhale deeply. This time, I let the water guide me.

I invite Wu Wei.

This ocean is my protector, and this time, I give myself permission to trust it.

As I inhale deeper, I allow the oxygen to stay in my body. I hold it a bit longer than normal. It begins to feel like ice freezing all my hot, steaming anger. I picture radiance, and I imagine an answer coming to me.

Wu Wei.

Suddenly, I realize the truth. The space I am looking for is already here. The physical space doesn't exist in prison (of course it doesn't!), but the spiritual space is always available for me. My breath can lead me there. That's what this ocean is.

"Who are you?" I hear my thirteen-year-old self ask again.

He doesn't know me, but he can. I can get to him. I know that I can. This space will guide me to him. This space is the only way in, and though I find myself stuck in this place without any room to breathe, I have somehow found my breath. My portable radio, a cheap piece of plastic from the early '90s, has become my gatekeeper.

I know that I can't escape the crowds of busy White men who wander around searching for meaning in all the wrong places. I can't turn off their noise, but I can sink beneath it. I can find meaning within my own body. I can be still in a world of noise.

I feel my hands loosening their grip on my radio. This ocean is not something I've made up. This ocean is very real; I am this ocean. I am the space that I need, and my Brown body holds enough space for me to be okay. My Brown body has navigated me through unsurmountable racism here, and incessant noise. I am learning to allow it.

Wu Wei is helping me allow what is. My breath is teaching me to go all the way into my body and to let go of everything else.

I think I can see the point now: meditation is an artform that can help me reawaken the noticing. The noticing in turn will lead to allowing, and allowing always leads to seeing. Meditation in prison is teaching me to go in — all the way into the body of who I was and into body of who I am.

I slide the volume dial back down on my radio, and I smile because I see the irony now. Through the static and white noise of my radio, in this White racist prison, I'm beginning to understand the power of my own Brown body.

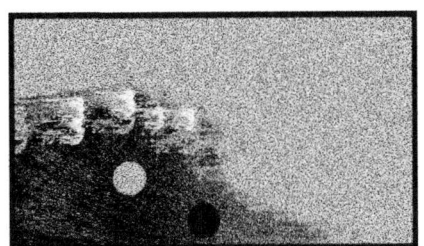

Meditation

Wu Wei invites us to participate in the ancient art form of stillness. It is a reminder to allow what is, which is not an easy task. Stillness and presence are quintessential truths that have become lost amid the busy patterns of our modern society. No, it is not cool or trendy to be still. Nevertheless, that is our task!

It will be an easy temptation to want to learn how to drop into the deeper meditations first – into the visual meditations within your own body – and avoid the simpler, more humdrum tasks required by the mindfulness of Wu Wei. I assure you, that will come, but not yet. Just as a skilled carpenter learns about the wood first before ever shaping it, so, too, must we learn to sit with our bodies — bodies needing to be held first, then understood, and later formed.

The how-to will come, but not yet. We must first learn stillness. We must first understand the shore we are on before we can set sail and arrive on another. People spend their whole lives learning to allow what is. This essentially is what enlightenment is: Being, itself.

The action of meditation is our yes response to the Universe's timeless questions to humanity: "Are you willing to be present in a world that consistently indulges in future anxieties and past failures? In a world raging in movement, are you willing to be still?"

Before stillness, Great loss

Before you can learn how to be still, you must first ask yourself, "Why am I not still already?"

From your very birth, there has been something wrestling within you, a subtle hinting, a beckoning whisper. This wrestling hints at a longing deep within your bones, but you can't quite put your finger on it. That's okay, this is the journey, dear friends.

Often, our bodies are not still yet because we know there is something else within us that stirs us into curiosity and question. We suffer from spiritual FOMO (fear of missing out). In our fear, we surround ourselves with anything we possibly can to convince ourselves we're doing it right. We fear ourselves into success, which is one of the greatest spiritual placebos that exists. Contrarily, stillness begins by letting go of the idea that we need to get it right in the first place. We call this experience failure, and failure is the great loss that we all must face.

Wu Wei, or allowing what is to be, comes only after great loss, not before. Without great loss, we are still stuck in the ego — a self that assumes it is the center of its own Universe. Trust me, there is no stillness there.

The ego can be described as having the following characteristics: needing to get things right, needing the approval of others, pointing out the faults of everyone else, self-identifying through achievements and accomplishments, black and white thinking (also referred to as dualistic thinking), feeling as though failure is not an option, believing that hedonism and materials are not separate from who we are, and living out of and acting from a fear-based energy.

Does this sound familiar?

In short, the ego is the smaller version of ourselves, which maintains the notion that we are separate from everyone else and everything else in the Universe. The ego maintains a posture that it should have some type of control or power over everything else around it. It is in this separateness that the ego thrives; its very life force depends upon its ability to compare itself to everything else around it.

As people, we are not so good at identifying the ego. At first, we are not even aware that our ego exists. A great loss must occur for us to glimpse outside of the small world we've always known. The discovery of something larger than ourselves is the beginning of the death of our ego. This death can take the form of anything that gets us outside of our small self. It might be a divorce, the loss of a parent, spouse, or child, a traumatizing car accident, being fired from a prominent position, declaring bankruptcy, losing a home to a fire or foreclosure, or — in my case — going to prison. More often than not, the death of our small selves comes in the form of the one thing we're most afraid of.

This death creates a small movement within us which shifts the dynamic of our thinking, and eventually, we land on a shore that asks us to let go of our thinking entirely. We begin to walk along a new sand, and with each step, we realize more and more that we were never the thing we always thought we were (the ego). Then afterwards, maybe, just maybe, we start to awe at the notion that we are a part of something much larger — the great unfolding. Prison, of course, was the beginning of my small death. It was the catalyst — the brick removed that caused the whole building to fall in on itself. My insight into Wu Wei could not have come to me in the way it did without experiencing the small death first.

A simple exercise to start

To start, I want to offer one simple question, and please, be easy with yourself.

Start by sitting in silence for five minutes. Then, when you are ready, I want you to ask yourself one question:

What am I most afraid of?

Be honest with yourself.

At first, it might be spiders or the dark. It might be a fear of public speaking, driving, or ghosts. But sit with it a while and be wholly honest with yourself.

What am I afraid of?

The truth is, our deepest fears come to us in the form of great loss, and it is through this great loss that we come to stillness. This is the only way to truly begin to know ourselves.

For now, be open to the possibility that what you are most afraid of won't actually hurt you. In fact, it might be the one thing that heals you in the end.

Oh, Brown body, you are a mountain.
Jagged and steep, full of danger and awe.
But this I know,
there is gold hidden in your hills.

Chapter Two

A Yin Yang Horse

A Zen student once asked his master what the key to understanding Zen was.

"How can I contain it? How can I grasp it?" he asked his master.

But the master remained silent. Instead, he led his student to a nearby river. There, he grabbed a pail and scooped up a bucket of water.

"Hold out your palms," said the master, breaking his silence. The student held out his palms and cupped them together.

Then the master poured the water into his student's palms. In moments, the water had seeped through the cracks of his fingers and spilled out onto the ground by his feet.

"You see?" the master said. "Is there a way to hold the water in our palms? Can we ever contain the water?"

The student shook his head.

"When you learn to hold the water in your palms, then you will understand Zen."

Each day, the master silently took his student to the nearby river. Again, each day, the master grabbed the same pail, scooped water from the river, and poured water in the palms of his student's hands. Each day, the water immediately spilled through and onto the ground.

"Tell me," the master said each time, "have you learned to hold the water in your palms today?"

"No," the student replied.

This went on for months.

One winter day, after the master and student arrived at the river, the master began to scoop water into the pale as usual, but then he noticed something strange. His student had begun to strip his clothes and was headed for the water.

Shivering in the cold, the student stepped into the freezing river. One step at a time deeper into the river, the student walked until he was up to his chest in water. With curiosity, the master spoke.

"What are you doing?"

Like usual, the student outstretched his palms and cupped them together, but then he lowered them and held his cupped palms underneath the water. Completely immersed, the student smiled. The master smiled back. This time, not a drop had spilled out.

The master humbly bowed toward his student.

"Rise out of the water. You now understand."

Eye contact is a funny thing in prison. It means something completely different.

In the West, it's a sign of respect, a sign of equality or power. In many Eastern countries, direct eye contact can be a sign of disrespect, so people there are taught to look away.

Though I was born in the East, I was raised in the

West. I was raised by a White family, in a White culture, with White customs. All I knew growing up were western concepts. I was raised to believe that looking someone in the eye meant you had nothing to hide. I remember being taught in school at a young age to look my teachers in the eyes. I learned it was a sign of respect; it showed them I was listening and attentive.

I grew up believing there was something shameful about looking down or looking away, so I always made a point to look people in the eyes. I must admit, there's a different kind of power in it, some kind of spiritual purity that takes place when you look another person in the eye.

I remember reading a theory involving reincarnation in one of my religious studies classes in college that always intrigued me — the theory was that everything in the end is reincarnated, except for the eyes because that's where the soul is. I've come to believe that there is a lot you can tell by someone's eyes.

But that's not the case in prison.

Prison is its own culture, so it comes with its own set of rules and customs. Prison is a place born of shame, and shame teaches you to look down. Prison is a place where the guards want you to look down. They don't want you to bother them. They don't want you to think you are equal to them.

Direct eye contact with a guard, or correctional officer (CO), can be taken as a threat. In prison, you get in trouble just for looking. I've learned pretty quickly that the same rules apply with other inmates. Here, you don't look people in the eyes unless you want to go pound for pound. I keep my head down mostly. I think there's too much sadness, too much pain, and too much guilt, so the men here hide their eyes behind their anger. There's a dull sadness in these men's eyes, but they don't want anyone to see it. They are too proud and too strong. Wolves don't cry.

There's a small part of me that empathizes with their sadness, but when I think about their blatant racism, my anger overpowers my empathy. The assaults never stop. I've never been punched because I'm smart. I don't go places where the punching happens, but I've been spit on many times. It often happens when my eyes are closed. It often happens when I'm meditating. The threats are usually empty, but I can still hear them through my headphones:

"Stupid sand nigger. Muhammad can't save you here. Better fucking watch yourself, punk."

When it happens, I can feel the anger pulsing in my body like a raging wildfire. The problem is it's always happening, so there's always fire. Maybe that's why my meditations bring the rain. Despite the anger, I try to keep still. I try to listen to the static of my radio, but their White-supremacist voices seem to overpower the white noise.

Over time, I've learned to make friends with my anger. We are now good roommates. I don't let my anger control me, but I also try to give my anger the needed space to feel. My anger reminds me there is more healing to be had. I can sense the healing waiting for me somewhere underneath all this pain. Anger is not a bad thing either. On many occasions, it has kept me alive. It reminds me to stay vigilant and to stay alert. My anger is a reminder of the constant injustice I face.

My anger is not my only beacon, though; my meditation is too. It reminds me that it's my responsibility to heal my own trauma and not point out everybody else's. Meditation in a place like this begs for insults, shame, and guilt. There's a saying for those in prison: Justice is *just us*. In my experience, loud, White men don't know how to handle quiet,

Brown men. People who can't sit with their thoughts don't know what to make of stillness, posture, and breathing. They jeer and taunt and hurl all kinds of insults. Despite the harassment, I persist, and at the very least, I do what I can to not make eye contact.

The insults and shame, hurt and danger, tend to stay in the body. That's what trauma is. It weighs the body down. I can feel each threat, each racist slur, each taunt, enter my body like a drug. It is viscous and feels like lead in my bloodstream. If it weren't for my meditation, I think I'd be so full of lead I'd sink to the bottom of my own soul and stay there.

Eye contact is powerful, and so is the body. I didn't grow up knowing that. The Christian culture I was a part of — and White American culture in general — didn't teach me anything other than to hate my body, to deny it, to distrust it, and to not delve deep within it.

"You'll get a new one in heaven someday."

"You don't need to trust yourself, just trust God, trust Jesus."

"When you do the right things, God rewards you."

But that God is not in prison.

Here, reward is not a reality, and trust doesn't exist. When you can't trust anyone, where do you go? My body has become my only friend, my only teacher. The more I begin to trust the words within myself, the more I begin to trust my body.

My body has become my teacher; my body has become my word. I'm learning that this word was God within me all along.

As a thirty-year-old Brown man in prison surrounded by White, angry men, I haven't had access to ideas like embodiment or generational trauma or self-love. Embodiment isn't available at face value here. Though I've read literature on embodiment from wonderful authors like Resmaa Menakem, Richard Rohr, Rupi Kaur, Yung Pueblo, Ram Dass, Bessel van der Kolk, Eckhart Tolle, and Wim Hof, I haven't had the same kind of access to that wisdom in prison. In a place like this, words can feel hollow even when they are beautiful.

It's harder to trust the beauty of the poets when you have bigots and xenophobes for background noise. In prison, I don't have TED talks, memes, or Instagram posts about deconstruction and reconstruction. In prison, all I have is myself. I have only come to know embodiment through the practice of embodiment. Because my body is the only thing I have here, I must learn to trust it; my poor Brown body — the thing that has caused so much pain and suffering in my life — is now becoming my teacher, in the Whitest place possible.

I close my eyes and turn my radio up. The static pierces through me like the first sip of a crisp cider. The static white noise wakes me into meditation. I pull my beanie over my eyes and sink down into myself. The radio static sounds like rain, which is the first image that comes booming into my mind. I know this rain can wildly change its course, as it often does.

I'm standing in a field with my mouth open skyward. The sound of rain purifies me. There's so much rain; I'm gulping it. The drops are warm like summer. I'm in a field that feels familiar. (I grew up on fifty acres. Maybe it's a field near my parents' farm, but I'm not sure.) It's an Oregon field, full of wet mounds of grass, mole hills, and soft soil. The static noise pounding into my body tells me to listen to it, listen to the rain as it gets louder.

Suddenly, I see a horse. It's a wild stallion. His coat is a dark brown, but he has a large white spot on his back — almost yin-yang like. The horse is drenched in rain. His mane is tangled and knotted. His eyes meet mine; they are wounded with wisdom. He stirs hot breath through his nostril, but he's not angry. His whinnying isn't a sound of warning but of peace. This wild yin-yang horse stands tall; he is inches from me. He nudges me with his nose, but it is a nudge of love. He is trying to get my attention.

I see his large muscles in front twitch. Horses wear the muscles of their body strong, and I can see every thew and sinew. I can feel every wince and twitch. For some reason, I feel connected to this horse, like it's trying to tell me something, like it understands a part of my past that I don't. He is standing so still, but his muscles are active in the rain. I hear a familiar voice inside me whisper:

Feel its muscles. Feel your own.

I place my hand gently on his mane, and I begin to stroke his neck. We are now connected. For a moment, we aren't any different from each other. I notice the stillness of this horse, but when he winces or whinnies, his muscles twitch. He stirs for a brief moment. First the front part of his neck shudders just slightly, and then the twitch moves toward the muscle below his neck. He winces again, stirs, whinnies, and then is still. This pattern happens several times. I can feel each pulse. I can feel his hot life running through him.

I look into his deep brown eyes and see my reflection

in his pupils. He sees me and gets me. Even in this meditation I am not used to looking things in the eyes. It's almost as if this horse is telling me it sees me. It's almost as if this stallion is challenging me to see myself, to go deep within my own body and look into my own eyes.

It's unsettling and uncomfortable, but I don't turn away. A few moments go by, and the unsettling begins to melt away like the snow in spring. Looking in the eyes of this stallion, I begin to understand a very small truth about the life force in all things: Nothing is permanent. We are all just here temporarily trying to figure it out, trying to connect. Suddenly, just like that, the stallion is gone, and I am left alone in the hard rain.

I'm not sure where he has gone, but I know the meditation has taken him. Now I am well aware of my own body. Somewhere, I can feel the pain of my back against the hard mat of the prison cot. I feel the cold metal beneath my spine. Like the stallion, my own muscles violently twitch. I can feel them pulsing.

Prison bunks are anything but comfortable. I move around all night, tossing and turning, grabbing at my own back, jabbing my fingers into the knots to try and ameliorate my pain, but I find no relief, not this time. This time, I am being told just to listen to the pain. I am being told to welcome it. I am still deep in meditation; I know I am because the static through my headphones still comes in the form of harsh rain. I am still in this field but well aware of my own body.

This is the first step to knowing myself, and it's taken me thirty years to do it. Why have I ignored my body for so long?

Men stay perched on their bunks. It's their only space, but the bunks are not comfortable. They squeak and move around. They're bent and uneven, and the mats are paper-thin with thirty-year-old stains from prisoners before us.

Mine have gang signs drawn into them from Sharpies. Sometimes when I'm meditating, I open my eyes for a moment, look down, and see the words "you motherfucker" written in Sharpie just below my legs. I can't help but laugh. The Universe can have a real sense of humor.

There's an inmate in here who likes to write things on my bunk and on my books. I'll come back from chow and see the word "nigger" written in Sharpie by my bedpost. When he walks past me, he shoves me with his elbow. He has a tattoo on his arm of Jesus hanging on a cross, but instead of a cross, it's a swastika. He grunts every time he walks by me, puffs out his chest, and flexes his arms. He has long, greasy hair and a few Aryan Brotherhood tattoos on his neck. His teeth are jagged like a vampire's, and he wears his hair in front of his eyes so no one can see him. For a while, he was my neighbor.

He made a point to shake my bed whenever he walked by me, or he'd throw my things on the floor. I never made eye contact with him or confronted him or even spoke to him. I just kept to myself and tried to mind my own business, but it didn't matter. He wanted trouble, and he was much bigger than I was. I'd come back from the yard to find my pillow on the ground or a book of mine in the garbage.

One night when I couldn't sleep, I got up to go to the bathroom, and I saw him there, sitting on his bunk, wide awake. He looked over at me, and for the first time, our eyes finally met. In that moment, I saw him for who he was: just a lonely, miserable, scared kid. And for that brief moment, he knew that I knew. He knew that I could see it in his eyes; I didn't have to say anything.

He never shook my bunk again.

Somehow, the wisdom of my body is instinctually guiding me to some deep, hidden knowledge about myself, and my body is using my meditation to get there. I have learned that when we sit with the pain of our body, we sit with the pains of the world. When we sit with the joys of our body, we sit with the joys of the world too. Our body is the key; our body is the footstool.

Beneath our layers of memories, aches, hurts, traumas, and moments of unfelt love, there is an energy waiting to transform us. The first step is to notice what is in our own body — notice the muscles, notice the way we sit, the way we stand, the way we feel when our necks turn a certain way or our fingers bend forward, notice the way our muscles feel when we lie outstretched or curled up or hunched over.

Through the wisdom of a yin-yang horse, this particular meditation is teaching me to listen to the muscles in my body, listen to their aches and hurts, because each one tells a story. My pain is being held in my body. Of course, where else could my pain be held? When you begin to take notice of what you hold, you begin to notice what has a hold on you. These spiritual patterns lie deep within us. These patterns, at the molecular level, shape who we are in very physical and spiritual ways. The first step is to notice them. This meditation is beginning to teach me not to be afraid to look into the eyes of my soul.

Our bodies hold patterns. We are creatures of habit, and our habits form our lives. If you don't believe me, just go to prison and see how quickly you create a routine. Then, notice how quickly you depend upon that routine, no matter how dull and dark it is.

The patterns are like muscles. The more we exercise these patterns, the stronger they get. In fact, the patterns are held within our muscles. The only way to recognize these patterns is to go into the body and become your body. You need to make friends with your body, get to know it and trust it. You need to make friends with each part of yourself.

No one had ever told me to listen to my body. The first time I learned to was from my own body, here in prison. I remember I turned on my radio; my body was calm, and my eyes were closed. I was breathing just fine, though under water. With each breath, I could feel a deeper voice inside me telling me to breathe. In the Christian tradition, I learned to ask myself the question, "Who am I?" In the Buddhist tradition, I learned to respond with, "Who's asking?"

When I began to ask the questions deep in meditation, I began, for the first time, to listen to those responses. Oddly enough, parts of my body would light up depending upon what the response was. If I was feeling fearful, I would feel parts of my lower back begin to light up, sending me signals of fearful energy. Sometimes, if I felt unsafe, my lower back would give me a little nudge, like the warning light on the dash of my Honda Civic. In western culture, we like to believe that things belong to us. My body. My spleen. My kidney. My stomach. Everything is mine, and it is an object for me to have control over. Spirituality of the body teaches you something different. Everything belongs. Everything is a part of something much larger than your own small possession of it.

Meditation has slowly taught me to see the different parts of my body like a group of friends, each person with their own unique relationship. I have learned under this sea of static to see these body parts as living organs, each holding its own pains and traumas and hurts. I have begun to see my stomach not as my stomach but as something alive that I could have a relationship with, something I could get to know. When I am deep in meditation, I can feel the different parts of me that need attention, and I talk to each part like an old friend. The static speaks to me here, deep in this field, soaked in the rain. *Listen to your muscles, listen to your body parts, they are trying to speak to you.*

By going into myself and sitting with myself, I am able to see the patterns within me. I am able to see how one destructive thought can lead to another. I am able to see how one action can lead to another action. Only in sitting with the body are we able to notice these hidden patterns within ourselves. First, though, we need to listen, and we need to begin to notice.

Just as the Zen student learned the only way to hold water in the palm of his hand was to immerse himself fully in the water, so, too, have I learned it is impossible to discover who I am without fully immersing myself inside my own body. You must go into the body and become your body — that is the key. You must be willing see with new eyes, in a way that pierces beneath the skin.

This is the only way you can really know yourself and notice the hidden spiritual patterns of your being. It won't matter how much you pray or meditate or how many rosary beads you pluck. It won't matter how many books you read or how many churches you attend. It won't matter how many followers you have on Instagram or how many of your yoga videos go viral on TikTok. If you don't go into your body, if you don't immerse yourself and become one with your own body, it will be like water seeping through the cracks of your fingers.

R.G. Shore

Meditation

Dear Friends,

How do we begin to know our body? Is it something that we own? Is it something we become?

Though it's the closest thing to us, for many of us, the body is the farthest thing away from us. For nearly thirty years, I had no idea what my body even was. I had no idea what my feet were doing when I wasn't walking. I had no idea what my stomach was doing when I wasn't eating; I had no idea how my body felt at all because I never bothered to ask for his opinion.

Before we can learn to sink deep into meditation, we must first get to know the patterns of our own body. We must be willing to form a relationship with the thing that has taken care of us our entire life. Just as I encountered the yin-yang horse in my meditation, I also encountered parts of myself that had long been neglected. For me, I needed to first observe something inside myself in order to learn how to observe the moving parts around me. I think the more we are able to notice and observe what's going on within, the more we are going to be able to discern what's going on without.

Before Change, Noticing

The change within you will happen, but it takes a subtle noticing first. Meditation and breathing teach us to slow down our movements. Observing one breath teaches us to pause before taking another. Learning how to notice the slow movements within us strengthens our ability to allow and accept the faster movements that make up our daily lives: Making a last-minute trip to the grocery store only to find they're out of the one ingredient you need. Being stuck in traffic at a red light when you're late for an important interview. Forgetting to take out the garbage on garbage day when you're already five minutes late for work. Folding the laundry just in time for the kids to come racing in and knock the clothes all over the floor. Seeing that gas has doubled in cost since last week, and you're stuck wondering how you're going to make it to work on an empty tank. Oh, and finding out you need a new roof just after learning the fridge no longer works, and it's only Monday.

These worries and anxieties are the faster movements that tend to entangle us. Like a spider weaving its web around a dizzied fly, our anxieties, worries, shames, and guilts engulf us in the endless spin. Noticing and observing is the first step to loosening the spider's deadly silk woven tightly around your chest. Only then will you finally be able to breathe.

Body Scan Exercise

A great way to begin noticing your own body and the energy patterns within you is by doing body scans before or after your meditation time.

What is a body scan?

A body scan is a slowing down exercise that helps you begin to observe what is going on within your body. Because I had so much time in prison being stuck on my bunk, I taught myself to go within. Over time, body scans became instinctual for me, and I became very good friends with the different parts of my body.

First, I encourage you to find a space to rest and

breathe. Take five minutes away from the busyness.

You can sit cross-legged, straight, with your spine erect, or you can lay down on the ground. It doesn't matter how you choose to sit, so long as you are in a comfortable position that allows you to notice and observe the different parts of your body. Often people make the mistake of trying to do it too perfectly. When you focus too much on getting it right, it becomes more stressful than relaxing, and you remain in your head instead of your body. Like the Wu Wei river, you should enter into its flow and go with the current, not against it. Remember, meditation is a kindness, so let it be kind to you.

Start by taking four deep breaths in and out and listen to the sound of your breath as you breathe in. Make sure to breathe into your gut, into the depth of your belly. Listen to the sound of your breath as you exhale. Notice the filling of your stomach and also the letting go. What does it sound like? A whistling? A whisper? A train? Just notice.

I encourage you to close your eyes. If you keep your eyes open, you might have too much visual stimulation, which can cause you to be outside your own body instead of in it. I have fallen victim to visual stimulation many times in my meditation journey, which is why I learned in prison to pull my beanie down over my eyes.

Start the body scan by focusing on your feet. It will be natural to want to think about your feet instead of observing how your feet feel. This distinction is important. In meditation, we let go of the thinking, and we become the process of becoming. In other words, when we think, we stay in the mind. So, do not think about each body part, become each body part.

Noticing is about forming a relationship with the energy you are noticing. In the West, we like to think things are subject to object — my kidney, my spleen, my body. Through meditation, I have learned that everything is subject to subject — everything has relationship.

Form a relationship with your feet. Form a relationship with your stomach, with your kidneys, with your spleen, with your lungs, with your heart. Start by asking how each part is doing. Like running into an old roommate from college, invite each part in for coffee. Get to know each part and ask how it has been.

On the other hand, the different parts of your body need to be able to trust you before they will open up, and that can take time. If I ran into my old roommate from college ten years later and randomly asked him to move in with me, he'd probably scream and run away. (Scratch that, I'd probably scream and run away.) The neglected parts of your body are the same, so don't press too quickly. Give them time to respond and get to know you.

Lastly, scan each body part, taking your time to move up your body. Sit with each part for as long as it takes, invite it in, let each part feel welcome and held. This helps to awaken the feeling and distances you from your thinking mind. I have learned you can never spend too much time with your body.

Try practicing this exercise over several months. Over time, you'll become more readily able to discern how each body part is feeling and responding. Being connected and in communication with the different parts of your body allows you to be gentler with them. Body scans are a great way to remind you to be gentle with yourself. In being gentler with your own body, you'll be gentler with others around you. I assure you, your body will thank you for letting it know you are listening in such a kind way.

My body is a warrior
my breath, its sword

Chapter Three

Exhaling the Ego

I close my eyes to center my breath. With the help of my radio, it comes like a hurricane. You cannot force your breath; you have to let it lead you. I have learned to experiment with different movements of breath. Before prison, I read a lot about the "Ice Man," Wim Hof, who uses cold and breath to go into his body. I read many of his books and watched many of his videos on YouTube. I learned to move into my breath through the cold. For a long time, I was disciplined enough to take daily cold showers. The cold really leads you right into your body. It stabs at all your hot, wasted thoughts. It washes out all the busy noise with its ice until the only thing that's left is the breath and the body.

In prison, however, warm showers are the closest thing to any kind of comfort, so I have stopped taking cold showers to enjoy the little luxuries I have. The concrete walls and floors and metal bunks are cold enough. Wim Hof teaches people to breathe into the belly, and he does it loudly and unabashedly. The last thing you want to do in prison, however, is bring attention to yourself, and breathing loudly can bring unwanted attention. There is no solitude here. There is no room for fire breath or deep, loud, belly breaths. When I meditate and chant "OM," I have to do it silently, too.

There is so much noise in prison. The routine, the anger, the violence — all of it can be too much. But in practicing meditation, I have learned to go inward and have begun to notice the patterns underneath the noise. Just like anything else, there are good days and bad days in meditation. Sometimes I can't shake the cacophony.

I close my eyes to meditate, but I can hear some of the inmates arguing from across the dorm. Their fierce language echoes their lifetime of hurt. Their constant bickering is like a moth, and my meditation, its flame.

I try to imagine the crashing waves, but I can hear the arguing grow louder.

"Nigger."

"Bitch."

"Motherfucker."

Men constantly blame others for their own hurts and pains. The damage of their words slides off their tongues so effortlessly. The words are meant to wound and punish, to shift blame and shift focus onto anything but themselves. It's a world they've always known, and it's a world I am now a part of.

The men are fragile here. They puff their chests like birds, but I can see what's going on under all their ruffled feathers. Beneath the faded swastika tattoos and the tough, leathery skin, I try to remember that there is a heart there too, and it beats like mine. The men are much larger than me. I am five-one (maybe five-two on a really good day). Their fists bang together like hammers. Though it would take but a moment to end me if they wanted to, I am not afraid. I understand now that these men are still children: lonely and completely unsure of who they are. When I get angry at their words, I try to picture their ten-year-old selves. I try to picture who they were as children, because it is easier for me to be kind to that part of them.

We are all searching for some kind of identity, and it's no different in prison. The tribalism that is so prevalent in our country today is condensed and concentrated here. The same desires that people have on the outside don't change when you get in here. We want to feel like we belong to something, and we cling to groups because groups give us a sense of security, a sense of belonging. America is a country of dualisms. We love "either/or" thinking: you are either with us, or you are with them. You are either a republican or a democrat, Christian or non-Christian, criminal or law-abiding, profitable or a liability. Duality in America teaches us you are either a success or you are a failure. Our egos like to compartmentalize things into the binary world of ones and zeros — it's cleaner and more efficient. Inmates are driven by the same ego thinking, but the tribalism is just more black and white... literally.

They call them "cars" because it's about who you ride with. The Blacks ride with the Blacks, the Whites ride with the Whites, the Mexicans (or Pisces) ride with the Pisces, and the Natives ride with the Natives. Everything is politics, and more specifically, skin color. Like I said, it's not any different in here than it is out there. You have to be tough in prison, but I can see the fragility underneath the forced *machismo*.

When I close my eyes, I see these men. I must admit that most times I don't want to. I yearn for a solitude that just doesn't exist here. I want just one moment to myself that I never can seem to get. I try to breathe deep — so deep that the sound of breath crashes over all the other sounds in the dorm like tidal waves. I pretend to hear and smell the profound peace of the ocean and its salt air with each breath, but the sounds and smells of harsh racism and cheap deodorant come wafting in instead. The contrast of my meditation set against the background of my incarceration is a paradox and an impossibility, but spirituality is a necessary impossibility.

Wisdom work means letting go of ego. Prison life is all ego, which makes the meditation difficult. Our egos like to be in control. Our egos like to drive the conversation, to tell the body where to go, and to tell the mind what to think. The ego is a muscle flexed habitually, and it can out curl any bicep. It is the child within us that was never heard, never fully understood. It wants to be right; it wants to be in charge.

In wisdom work, we call it "shadow." You must get to know your shadow and understand who it is and why it acts the way it does. America is an ego-driven country, urging us to constantly get it right; America is all shadow. It is a country defined by winners and losers, and the ego hates to lose. In contrast, people in prison have never gotten anything right. They have never won, which complicates the way the ego works. For many of these men, they have never been successful a day in their life. Most never graduated high school, maintained employment, or had lasting relationships. Many can't read, spell, or carry healthy conversations. When we have very little experience with winning, we create reasons in our minds to justify treating everyone else like losers. The Brownness of my skin here makes me a loser. My education makes me a loser. My yin-yang tattoo makes me a loser. My knowledge of the law makes me a loser. My failures make me a loser.

The ego is a ladder, each rung successfully reached propels you upward. In America, we are conditioned from a young age to climb — no matter the cost — from diploma, to bachelor's degree, to master's, maybe a Ph.D., to a pretty family with a beautiful home and a dog that fetches the frisbee. The American ego insists we keep climbing upward in status and image. How far must we climb? Do we own our own business someday? Do we make six figures? How many houses do we own? How many followers do we have on Instagram? How many of our TikTok videos have gone viral? I am reminded of Thomas Merton's masterfully crafted thought on the ego. It's like climbing a ladder your whole life only to realize the ladder is leaning against the wrong wall. What are you to do but jump?

The status of our climb is measured by the people on the rungs below us and the people on the rungs above us, but there are so many factors that determine how far we can climb and what rung we start on. In prison, there is still a ladder, but it runs horizontally.

Being marginalized greases our hands — from the color of our skin to our gender, sexual orientation, socio-economic status, class, and, of course, our criminal history. With so much grease between our fingers, slipping from the ladder is an inevitability. The more I go into my meditation, the more time I spend in my body and with my body, the more I realize how much my Brownness has explicitly affected my stature in life. Being Brown and being incarcerated has a direct effect on my ego, reminding me of my own fragility and my own humanness. I must admit, I am just as fragile as everyone else.

When I go into my body, I feel the hurt. I feel my wounds opening. I feel how different parts of my body hold these pains, anchoring me to the weight of my guilt within me and the weight of my shame for feeling like I just never got it right. It's harder to accept the pattern when the only pattern you've known is death. It's harder to let go of getting it right if you feel like you've never got it right in the first place. But meditation is not about getting it right. I admit I struggle with letting that go too.

Meditation has taught me that you can't both seek truth and be right. The two are in opposition of each other because one is rooted in freedom and the other is rooted in ego. Unfortunately, I have found that most people would rather be right than seek truth. The former is an easier path, full of blaming and fear and justification. The latter requires you to move inward and face the parts of yourself you need to face: there is just no other way to heal.

I have found that, most often, people aren't willing to face their shadow until they're put in a situation where they no longer have access to the sun. Meditation is not about getting it right or looking a certain way, which is why modern meditation through the algorithms of social media can be so dangerous. Often, the meditation we are exposed to daily spits out a formula opposite of its original intent. It's not about getting it right or looking good but letting go of the desire to do it right or the desire to look good.

Yet, if the patterns are working for you, why change them? That is why there are so many rich but unhappy people.

That is why the gap between those who have and those who don't have is only widening in our society. If the image looks good, then there's no reason or incentive to change it. Only when that image or that success fails us do we begin to realize maybe there's something more to life than how many likes our photo got on Instagram or how many times our tweets were retweeted. Spirituality is a ladder that asks us to climb down into God, not up.

So, down the ladder I go.

I lay here in frustration flexing my ego muscle. It's hard to let it go and swim underneath it, but I know that I need to. Exhaling the ego allows for the inhaling of freedom, or something that feels like it. It's hard to grasp your own failure when you're constantly drowning in it. It's like trying to chomp on your own teeth. Slowly, the meditation muscle is training me to let go of the ego muscle.

I put my headphones over my ears.

Breathe deep, I tell myself.

Don't let the ego win. Just allow what is to be. You can't control anyone else's actions but your own.

I lay down on my bed and fiddle with the switch, flipping from radio station to radio station. Besides old country music and the occasional classic rock song, there is only static. I lay on my bed and listen to it. Slowly, the radio begins to sound like natural sounds of the earth, like rain or flowing water. It's calming. I close my eyes and synchronize my breath with the sound of the white noise. Soon, I see a vast ocean in front of me. The waves are crashing up against the jagged rocks. The swells grow large. I'm standing on a large rock, and the waves are coming all the way up to my feet. Amidst the swirling of tumultuous water, I see a cool pond in front of me, a circular area carved out in the rocks, where calmer water has been trapped. I head toward the pond and climb up over the rocks. Looking down, I notice that I'm barefoot. My feet and the jagged rocks are connecting — the Earth and I are one. The waves continue to crash behind me, the sound of white noise hitting my ear drums through my prison headphones.

I reach the edge of the tide pool; it looks inviting. The water is deep but still shallow enough I can see the bottom of the pond with fish swimming below. As I peer in, I see an island of small rocks on the bottom of the ocean floor; the rocks are covered in anemones. Without hesitation, I jump in with a splash. The water is cold. I dunk my head underneath the water. Immediately, the sounds of crashing waves and radio static become muffled. It's peaceful under the water, and I can breathe down here. Stay down here, I find myself saying. You can breathe. Remember, this is a meditation. It's safe down here. You can stay.

So, I stay.

When I'm in deep meditation, I can see my whole body. It's relaxed, and I'm looking at it from the outside. Because I use the visualization of water, I'm usually floating, which gives me a sense of peace and lightness. Only after a while do I begin to feel my body inviting me in. None of my body is touching the earth now. I and the water are fluid.

I decide to swim deeper.

Down on the ocean floor, I watch the anemones on the rocks expand and contract. Are they breathing? I'm not sure, but I get the urge to touch them. They look like underwater kiwis. I put my finger in the middle of the anemone and watch it contract around my finger. It feels sticky and muscular as it tightens. I quickly pull my finger out and watch the anemone relax and expand again. It moves so elegantly underneath the water.

Now, I can sense the anemone is trying to show me something about myself. It's trying to get me to see the patterns within me. What pattern am I supposed to see? I poke at the anemone one more time, and the same thing happens. Its gummy center wraps around my finger and pulls it in. The water is quiet around me, and my body is still. What am I supposed to see? I ask myself. What is this meditation teaching me? And then I hear a familiar voice.

Notice. Just notice.

So, I do.

I wade here underneath the water. I breathe in and out and look around me. The water is cool; thousands of tiny bubbles float past me. Small seaweed and kelp float gently with the bubbles. Suddenly, my eyes dilate, and I see this underwater view with a clearer lens.

Everything is large.

Everything is moving together.

The seaweed. The water. The bubbles. The anemones. The fish.

It feels like one large organism — all connected.

I watch the anemones breathe in and out. They are breathing just like me, but they are doing it effortlessly, without anger or resistance.

I think about my ego. I think about the muscles of my meditation. I think about how I undulate between the two, pulsing back and forth between my ego self and my true self. I think about how much resistance I feel between the two. When I poke at my shadow, when I prod at my spirit, when I try to figure it all out, I can tell my inner being contracts and tightens around me, not letting me in. What were to happen if I stopped poking, I wonder.

Then I realize it: just as inhaling and exhaling are necessary for breathing, undulation between ego and spirit is necessary for allowing. Allowing the wound to exist leads to the healing. Without the wound, there wouldn't be a need to heal, and without the ego, there wouldn't be the gravitational pull toward a deeper energy. They both exist, and there is no need to prod at either of them. The ego is a mirror that reflects the shameful parts of us, the parts we don't want anyone to see. The deeper energy of the Universe is a mirror that reminds us that everybody is looking into the same mirror (and that the mirror doesn't matter anyway).

People in prison have fingers pointing at them all the time. The triggers are endless. People in here have failed so explicitly according to society's standards; they are constantly being prodded and poked at like anemones being poked by a plethora of fingers. The ego is so fragile that all it knows how to do is contract and tighten and defend itself from the thing that's threatening it. But being defensive and closed up leaves no room or space for true healing. Being defensive leads us away from the allowing, which is necessary for true growth.

The truth is our society and culture don't want to see people heal; they want to see people blamed. Blaming others always allows us to keep our own fragility at bay. So, where is the real wound? Why are people so hesitant to allow a path of healing for those that are seeking it? What rights do inmates have? Do we have the right to heal? To move forward? To breathe? To find love? To be human?

While the ego loves losers and winners, the Universe reminds me that through the energy of its love, we all deserve to be winners. It is the truth. No matter what we have done or what we think about ourselves, we are all being held in something much more powerful than our own small, fragile selves. We are being held in a larger organism that is all connected — moving and breathing as one. And this thing that connects us, asks that our *whole* selves heal, not just parts of us.

The more I sit under this ocean, the more I realize the finger poking the anemone is me. I am prodding at myself. It's my ego; it's my sadness, my loneliness, and my shame. Power does not lie with the people that oppose us but in the energy we let those people have. The power I possess to embody who I really am lies in the energy I am willing to give myself. It does not lie with these prisoners around me, just as it does not lie with people poking at me from the outside.

I hear the voice again.
Just notice, notice how you feel.

At first, I get angry. Anger is my protector. I thrash around underneath the water, almost losing my breath. What is underneath all that anger? I pause and begin to notice myself. I begin to notice how I really feel. There are buzzworthy feelings, and then there are the real vulnerable feelings. This water is encouraging me to embrace my own vulnerability, no matter how painful it feels. Loneliness, rejection, abandonment — these are feelings no one likes to admit they are feeling, and yet, I feel them all the time. These are not cool feelings. These are not trendy feelings I can go live on Facebook and talk about.

Society teaches us that it's unsafe to be vulnerable, so, we learn to poke and prod at these feelings. We learn to manipulate and twist ourselves into feeling differently, because we've been taught that the other feelings are more acceptable. We've been taught that the vulnerable feelings are just a waste of time. Society teaches us to be tough. Society teaches us to be busy and to appear to be in control: "Suck it up," "Be a man."

We are tempted with so many distractions and so much anger. Very rarely do we give ourselves permission to feel the lonely, isolated, rejected, and abandoned feelings underneath. However, meditation brings you right down into it and asks you to sit with it. Like getting into an ice bath, it feels like a thousand daggers jabbing into your skin. Your whole body screams at you to jump out of the water, which you instinctually want to do. But if you just pause and allow — if you begin to feel and observe the feelings underneath all that pain — you begin to see that there is something fuller underneath, and it's begging you to listen to it. It's begging you to let it heal.

Chapter Four

A Universal Life Force

I'm lying in my bunk with my eyes closed. The light peering through the window keeps bouncing off the back of my eyelids, changing from royal purple to fiery orange. There is a slight breeze, and as the curtains move, so, too, does the reflection of light. First, I hear the breeze. It's subtle, like a whisper, and then the light changes on the back of my eyes. As the curtain opens with the breeze, I see a brighter orange, and then as it closes, I see a deeper purple. Orange to purple, orange to purple — it's a pattern. I make ticking noises with my tongue, like a human clock to try to match when I think the back of my eyelids will change colors again. Tick — orange, tick — purple, tick — orange again.

Over time, I focus more on the colors, and I go into them. When I'm still enough, still in my body and in my mind, I see beyond the orange; I see beyond the purple. In between the layers of colors, I begin to see shifting patterns of the most intricate designs, like twisting kaleidoscopes filled with the most dazzling colors. If I stare too long or concentrate too hard, they disappear, and then it's back to fiery orange or royal purple. But for a slight moment, there is something else hidden underneath. Tick — mystery — tick.

Underneath, my skin is a tapestry of memories, traumas, and wounds all intricately woven together. They bounce around in me like the light bouncing off the curtain. Sometimes these wounds are too heavy to absorb. When that happens, the light within me is refracted, I lose my breath, my eyes open, and I'm back in the dorm. Meditation isn't an escape from reality, though. Rather, it is the choice to enter into a deeper one. When I meditate here on this bunk, sometimes it's me trying to get away from the danger of prison, but most times, it's just about me wanting to seek a deeper something within.

I first started noticing the lights long before prison. These intricate patterns of lights have followed me all my life. It's not the same kind of light you see when you stare at the sun too long or when oncoming cars forget to turn off their brights. No, this is a different kind of light. It holds an energy saturated with meaning.

When we were little, my brother and I used to take our tent and go camping somewhere in the woods of our parent's farm. We'd pack up our tent, sleeping bags, and all the other essentials of pre-teen adolescence: skittles, check; pillows, check; flashlights, check; Mountain Dew, check; War Heads, check.

After setting up camp, my brother and I would tell ghost stories to scare each other. We'd use the flashlight to magnify the looks on our dumb faces. We'd play truth or dare, which was just stupid, because it was only us two, but we still had fun. My brother would dare me to eat as many skittles as possible and chug all the Mountain Dew, and I would dare him to moon the moon, which we thought was the funniest thing. Then, when the excitement settled and we got into our sleeping bags, we would start to listen to the quiet of the farm. The natural sounds of the earth were humming with aliveness. We could hear coyotes banter in the distant hills, howling at one another, and the crickets buzzing in sync somewhere in the grass fields. Sometimes we'd hear owls up in the trees or the distant fluttering of bats. Even the moon seemed to gently whisper to us as she illuminated her rings in the dark blanket of the sky. My brother would fall asleep first every time, and then it would just be me — alone with the sounds of the night, alone with my thoughts.

I remember squirming around at first, trying to get comfortable in my sleeping bag, grabbing a handful of Skittles for good luck, and dunking my head deep into my pillow to find solace. But when I put my head down, my pillow didn't provide me the darkness and quiet I was looking for. Instead, I had entered a realm of lights: bright neon splashes of color, dazzling with patterns and glowing with life. They were blinking like stars but clothed in the most beautiful colors: hues of blues brighter than any blue I could describe, hot pinks, oranges, reds, and greens. The lights were buzzing around each other, floating in some kind of harmony. What was this world I had entered? A secret world of lights all within the confinement of my own pillow! I knew I was seeing something hidden beneath the normal images that make up everything around us. Somehow, I was catching a glimpse of the threads beneath the fabric.

It wasn't just a world within the confines of my pillow, because when I lifted my head in the darkness of the tent, the lights were still there, dancing around the night. Periodically throughout my life, I would see these same lights. They often comforted me and reminded me I was not alone. Sometimes they'd stay for long periods of time, and other times they were more ephemeral. I'd blink and see them, blink again, and they'd be gone. I wasn't sure exactly what these lights were, but one thing I did know — they held a deeper meaning and deeper truth to the existence of the Universe.

Some of my own digging and research over the years suggests that these lights could be biophotons: light particles generated within the body that are constantly emitted and radiated outward. Some research shows that meditation decreases the amount of biophotons emitted from the body, suggesting that biophotons could be somehow related to Qi energy or Prana. (The medical field calls this phenomenon coherent biophotons.) Regardless of what it's called, or even what it is, I've learned it has stayed with me and exists within me. I have learned that I have access to these lights wherever I go, even in prison.

As I wrestle around in my bunk here in the dorm, the fiery oranges and royal purples continue to bounce off my eyelids. I know I am being invited to just sit with the colors. When we just sit with our bodies and sit with our breath, we give ourselves space. Our bodies are begging for space all the time — space to move around and feel free, space to explore, and space to grow. This space is an internal space, of course. Our thoughts and our worries are like too many branches on a tree, blocking any chance of sunlight getting through.

My thoughts are intrusive. They wrangle me; they seize me all the way down to the bone. It starts with one thought, and before I know it, I'm 1,000 thoughts deep. It's like scrolling through Instagram: You can never look at just one post. The key is to allow the thought to be what it is, and at the same time, not follow it down the river. Let it float past you like a fish in a stream. You don't stare at the fish, but instead watch a spot in the water. Eventually, the fish will swim out of view.

The lights in my body are a signal for me. They center me. They ground me and remind me to be present. When I go into the body, that's when I begin to feel these lights. You can call it God or Divine Presence. You can call it Spirit or Mother Earth. Sometimes I call it the Universe, sometimes I call it Source. I call it multiple things just so I don't get too attached to any one name. This universal life force is an energy flowing within me, and this energy is calling me to discover a stillness underneath.

In the Taoist tradition, they call it life force, or Qi (chi). When Dr. Usui discovered it in the late 1800s, he called it Reiki (ki is pronounced like chi). In Hinduism, they refer to it as Prana, and in the Christian tradition, they call it the Holy Spirit, or Breath of God. I have learned it doesn't matter what you call it. The name isn't as important as the thing itself. A swimmer is a swimmer because they love the water, not because they love the temperature of the water. If someone is too concerned about the name of the thing, perhaps they aren't in love with the thing itself, but rather the culture to which that name was birthed. As the Dalai Lama says, if you go down deep enough, you begin to see that the roots of your tree touch the roots of all other trees. It is not necessary to get so attached to our own individual tree.

The truth is, there is a universal life force or life principle of energy within us, all of us. This same energy is the energy that makes up the entire universe. We are all little universes, I think. When I meditate, I try to remind myself that these energies live within me and they live in the stars, too. They meet us in the micro, and they meet us in the macro. These energies flow within me, and they come to me in the form of light. While most of it is a mystery, I believe these energies within me are guiding me to something so much deeper than the form of my body or the circumstances I find myself in. These energies are like a river, ever flowing within me.

But I still wonder, if the energies are like a river, what is the water?

I close my eyes and sink beneath the orange and purples. I breathe deep into myself. I feel my breath go down my throat and into my gut. I feel it move around in my belly, and I notice the way the energy lights up in those particular parts. The energy feels like a sun concentrated on one part of my body, like a heat lamp on a succulent. I breathe into that part, and I call upon my breath to lead me. Within moments, I'm underwater again. The ocean of my breath has led me there. My body somehow is floating peacefully, but this time, there is nothing under the water. It is just me, my body, and this sea of water surrounding me. I am breathing calmly, and my arms are floating softly, moving with the gentle flow of water. Parts of the water are illuminated dark blue and other parts are pitch black. I'm not afraid of this darkness, though. As I breathe in, I tell myself to go down deep within me. I can feel my body go inside itself. Deeper and deeper I go.

Suddenly, I am back at the lunchroom cafeteria, the same one as before. I'm staring at my thirteen-year-old self. He sees me and recognizes me from an earlier meditation, but he still doesn't know who I am.

"Can I sit?" I ask.

"Sure" he says, shrugging his shoulder.

His arms are still gangly, and his Quicksilver sweatshirt is too baggy for his body. His hair has pockets of brown dyed into its curls. He's smacking his gum loudly.

"Do you know who I am?" I ask him.

"Am I supposed to?" he responds.

I sit and watch him quietly. This is not a memory, this a meditation. I am having a real conversation with my younger self, and he doesn't know me. He doesn't recognize his older self, staring blankly at him from across the lunch table.

"I am sorry," I say.

"For that thing on the top of your head? Yeah, me too," he jokes sarcastically, referring to my current man bun.

I smile at him; he's so cool. He's so calm and collected. He knows exactly what to say. His survival instincts are perfect. He's been doing it for thirteen years straight, and he'll do it at least another seventeen. He knows what to say and how to say it. He knows how to read a room perfectly. He knows how to make people laugh quickly. He knows how to make people feel comfortable enough, while also keeping them at arm's length.

I want to protect him from all the shit he's about to go through over the next seventeen years. I want to save him and tell him about all of it. I want to warn him, but I don't know how. All I manage to offer is a sanitized commiseration.

"I am sorry that your life is so hard."

"Isn't it for everyone?" he responds defensively.

Some say there are three responses to trauma: fight, flight, or freeze. I remember a therapist telling me about a fourth response, fawn. The fawn response is a coping mechanism for those who feel so unsafe they develop a hyperawareness of people pleasing. They develop skills that help them survive by reading a room perfectly. They can keep everyone at bay. They people please because they think they need to earn love — that it's the only way. The fawn response comes from not feeling safe enough or loved enough. It can often be seen in children who have been rejected, abandoned, or abused.

I can see the fawn in my younger self. I can see how good he's become at reading a room. I can see how good he's become at saying exactly what he needs to say to be funny enough, smart enough, likable enough, without ever having to be vulnerable at all. After all, he's a Brown kid in a White world.

I see his hurt, but I don't know what to say, because his hurt is my hurt. And I don't know how to deal with my own hurt. It's too much at this point. Suddenly, I feel the hot anxious sensation on the back of my neck, like I want to get out of this meditation. I want to flee. I want to wake up in the shitty racist dorm above me — yeah, I'd even rather be there. Then, there is a whisper:

Just stay.

I hear a familiar voice tell me.

So, I wait. I sit down deep in my body, deep in this meditation. I pretend this is just an ice bath…an ice bath I can do. I can manage the cold.

Then I see them, the same dazzling lights I saw camping with my brother. They are floating across my old middle school cafeteria right in front of me, filling my body with new breath. Like the first sip of coffee on a sleepy morning, the lights begin to fill me with warmth. They are guiding me, reminding me it's okay, reminding me I'm not alone and I'm safe.

I look back at my younger self; his eyes are staring into mine with curiosity.

"Wait, you see them too?" he asks, referring to the lights.

"Yes," I respond. "Yes, I do."

"I thought only I could see them," I hear him tell me.

Then, deep within this meditation, I feel myself say the most unexpected thing to him.

"Do you want to get out of here?"

"Split a piece of wood and I am there.
Lift up the stone,
and you will find me there."
—The Gospel of Thomas, Ln 77

Chapter Five

A Divine Conversation

Everything is outside looking in. We are birds in cages here, and our perspectives are limited. On clear days, I can see the ocean at a distance, which is not too far away in the PNW, but seeing the ocean without being able to smell it is a punishment in itself. Sometimes when it's stormy, I convince myself I can hear the waves, but I know it's just the snores of inmates echoing through the dorm. The window next to my bunk is blocked by fir trees, which are outside the fence. I can't touch them; I can only see them. The light peers in through the window next to my bunk and heats the books on the windowsill.

You can't read the books in prison. Most of the pages are torn out because the inmates use them for joints. I learned that the hard way when I got to the last chapter of The Firm. The Bible's pages are thinner and make for the best rolling papers. I hear Ephesians is hard to read these days. I laugh because people are literally getting high on the Word.

Men in here stick to what they know and what they are used to. It's all about routine. The same men grease their hair with the same pomade. They scoop handfuls of what can only be described as pink lard and knead it into their hair like flour into dough. Every Monday new sheets come in, and we're required to get up early (sometimes as early as 4 a.m. to get the clean ones). The sheets are paper-thin and impossible to keep tucked in. The only way to keep your sheets on your bed is to tie them, which is against the rules, but it doesn't matter. Everybody does it. A lot of the sheets are brown: it's a combination of sweat and rust from the bunks.

For many of the men in here, prison is just as comfortable a place as any. It's what they know, and because it's what they know, it's predictable. People cling to predictability as much as they cling to their physical routines. Every Thursday is pizza day. A riot doesn't happen because an AB (Aryan brother) calls a Pisa (term for a Latino in prison) a punk ass; a riot happens because someone changes the menu, and there's no longer pizza on Thursdays.

The inmates need tangibility. They need something they can feel, touch, see, and wave around to others. Self-discovery is too internal, and self-love is too ethereal. Salvation is only for the Whites, and meditation is for the weird (as I'm often reminded). Sitting on your bunk, closing your eyes, and searching for stillness just doesn't really earn you the street cred you think it would. On the other hand, newfound religion tends to work for people in here. It's tangible and controllable. It can get wearisome being surrounded by so much religious narcissism, but I try to find the humor where I can.

Some of the men have Bible studies on Sundays, but you have to be the right race — and you have to be willing to tithe. Usually, a Cadillac gets you a seat in their church. (A Cadillac is a Milky Way candy bar and a coffee with milk and creamer added to it.) It's not far off from the way churches on the outside operate. There's always a bouncer at the door; there's always some kind of cover charge.

I once watched a Black guy, who went by the name Peanut Butter, walk by a table of White supremacists, and jokingly tell them they were praying to the wrong god. (Peanut Butter was the only Black guy who the Whites seemed to tolerate.)

"Them Bibles ain't gonna help you none. You know you all praying to the wrong god, right?"

"Yeah? How you figure Peanut Butter?" responded one of the guys at the table.

"For starters, you in here White boy," said Peanut Butter. "Second off, your cross is broken, it's supposed to look like a 't,' but all them corners is bent," PB chuckled, referring to the Swastika drawn in Sharpie on the front of the bible. "I'll let you in on a little secret tho. You gotta pray to Howard."

"Who the fuck is Howard?"

"Who the fuck is Howard? Come on, Nigga, you know, Howard! Our Father, who aren't in Heaven, Howard be thy name!"

Peanut Butter chuckled at his own humor and walked out of the room. I then watched one of the White guy's begin to chuckle to himself too, until he got a few stares from his not-so-happy buddies. I also couldn't help but laugh, quietly from my bunk of course. Peanut Butter had a point. Maybe I needed to be praying to Howard too. (I never did try it.)

Religion in prison is a lot like religion in the rest of America: it's fast-food. It's more about getting as much as you can as quickly as you can. There's no stillness underneath it. The men lose it as quickly as they find it. Like on the outside, religion tends to be more about being a part of a culture than about spirituality itself. Like on the outside, it's all about fitting in and playing the role they want you to play. Christianity in here is more about Bible roulette, proving people wrong, and born-again rhetoric than it is about any kind of transformation. More often than not, when people find God in prison, it's a god that looks a lot like them. I have found this sentiment to be true in America in general.

These same men who find God in the morning, forget it all by the afternoon. It's more about instant gratification than it is about seeing things in a different way. These are not issues in themselves, nor judgments. These are just signs of broken men trying to hold onto anything they can. After all, when you're stranded at sea, even a piece of seaweed can look like a good oar from far away.

When I think about religion in here, much as religion out there, I can't help but sense a hollowness within me and within these men. God seems to always be out there, just out of reach. For many people, God is a noun that can solve your problems and make sense of things that don't actually make sense. When you're desperate and looking for answers, you can find them almost anywhere. It's like looking at the shapes in clouds and seeing what you want to see. (I think they call it pareidolia.) You can make any shape out of a cloud if you want to, just like you can make any meaning out of a Bible verse.

You can tell people God told you to do something, and if you have enough Instagram followers, money, power, or political influence, you can probably get away with it. But like a Rorschach test, how you define God tells someone more about you than it does about God.

I've learned that the macro is always a reflection of the micro. Patterns echoed at the cosmic level are the same patterns within our own body. Divine Energy is everywhere. It took me a long time to see it within myself because the spirituality I was exposed to growing up promulgated a different kind of narrative.

Like the needles on the fir trees outside my window, God was always out there — just out of my reach. Growing up, God was a rigid mystery: his love was unknowable, but his punishment was predictable. I always found it odd that God was love...until you did the wrong thing. The narrative was that God was elsewhere — certainly not within my own body. Worship was an external posture, not an internal discovery. In fact, Christianity didn't include your body at all.

Growing up in the PNW, I couldn't help but feel somehow like that God didn't include me at all, no matter how much I prayed or tried to follow along. I was told by evangelical circles that God loved everyone equally...except women, because they couldn't lead a church or a family, and not Muslims or illegal immigrants. I was told that God died for everyone, but not the gays and certainly not trans people. Pastors continually preached that God's love was unconditional, but the idea of unconditional love wasn't something that seemed to actually be put into practice by the people preaching it:

First off, you had to believe in God. Though a logical conclusion, it still sounded like a condition to me.

Second, you had to believe in their version of God: still a condition.

Third, Jesus had to be savior: condition (Usually a condition that involved the bizarre and heady explanation of Substitutionary Atonement Theory).

Fourth, you had to read your Bible: condition.

Fifth, you had to go to church: condition.

Sixth, you had to evangelize (tell people about God), especially the homeless: condition.

Seventh, you couldn't have sex before marriage, or masturbate — ever: A pretty big condition (especially for a teenager).

Eighth, ninth, tenth, and eleventh, you couldn't drink alcohol, smoke weed, believe in any other kind of religion, or believe that anyone else was going to heaven, except for people who believed in Jesus: condition, condition, condition, and condition.

Twelfth, you had to believe that the Bible was literally true: condition.

Thirteenth, you had to make sure to deny your temptations at all costs, especially temptations of the flesh, because the body was somehow bad or evil or something. In fact, you had to believe the whole thing was shit the day you were born (original sin): condition.

Fourteenth, you had to be pro-life and, somehow, be pro-war at the same time: weird conditions. Abortions were bad, period — there was just no arguing that.

And finally, you had to believe that hell was an actual

place and heaven was only for the chosen or predestined: condition.

The more time I spent in Christianity, the more I realized God's unconditional love was, in fact, very conditional. The more time I spent being a Christian, the more I realized it had very little to do with discovering God as love and much more to do with making sure whatever love I discovered still met all the church's social requirements. It wasn't transformation; it was tribalism.

Here in prison, the conditions for being a Christian follow a similar trajectory. The rules for Christianity on the inside follow the same pattern on the outside, but they get even stranger. (I once heard a guy reading his Bible in here tell another guy that God forgives you if you become a Christian, but not if you're Black.)

Prison Christianity conditions:

You can't be gay, bisexual, or trans: condition.

It's okay to steal, but not from other Christians: condition.

If you're born again, you better preach it, obnoxiously: condition.

You have to be baptized by another Christian, again, preferably a White one: condition. (I once heard an inmate tell another inmate that baptism doesn't count if the guy who baptizes you is Black. I wonder if he knew Jesus looked more like me than he did like him…)

It's preferred that you're White, but some other races are tolerated — sometimes: condition.

Like being White, being saved is a rite of passage — a rite controlled by whoever has the most power — meaning, you must be willing to do what those in power say: condition.

You have to tithe, but the money always goes to the

leader of the group or the guy that baptized you: condition.

And apparently, though not explicitly spoken, you must believe that Jesus was White too: condition. (Unfortunately, another common belief shared amongst many evangelicals in our country.)

I'm not against Christianity. I just wonder how much transformation there actually is in the whole thing. Growing up Christian in the Pacific Northwest, I realized that I was accepted as long as I believed in the God Christians believed in. But their God always looked like them…and they were always White, and I couldn't look like them because I wasn't White enough to be White.

Perhaps Christianity in America is a reflection of America, not Christ. The hurt and frustration underneath this Brown skin of mine is that I just never could really fit into the culture Christians wanted me to be a part of. In my experience, Christian culture equaled American culture, and American culture, more often than not, seemed to equal White culture. The truth is, Jesus wasn't American, and he wasn't White either.

I remember in college getting into an argument with a pastor who told me I was wrong for wearing a yin-yang necklace as a Christian. He told me Jesus didn't wear a yin-yang necklace. I told him Jesus probably didn't wear a cross necklace either.

The pastor responded that it's what Christians do in America: they wear crosses.

I responded that Jesus wasn't American. In fact,

Christianity wasn't American. Though I admit I was anything but humble in college, I made a fair point: the pastor was more concerned about looking American than he was about looking Christian, or perhaps an amalgamation of the two. Maybe to him, the two were the same thing. No matter what I did, I just seemed to rub up against Christianity. In college, all I wanted was to belong, but it seemed no matter how hard I tried, I couldn't.

I know a lot of my reflections on Christianity are a projection of my own hurt ego. They are also a reflection of my body wanting some kind of control over the wounds inside me. I can also admit that my anger is a defense mechanism for what's really going on underneath all this hurt. The truth is, there are a lot of wonderful, life-transforming people who identify as Christian. And, I also know it's okay to feel hurt, and it's okay to feel the anger from my experiences. It's also okay to say that Christianity fucked me up.

It's important to acknowledge hurt right where it is. It's important to acknowledge a lot of really good people have been burned by Christianity too. It's no different in prison. The men in here who call themselves Christians are really angry and prideful, and they seem to be holding onto wounds that go a lot deeper than their anger. Prison has a funny way of helping you identify your hurts, while at the same time, reinforcing them. Again, the trauma is always dished up twice as fast.

As I sit here on this bed, I am learning that all I can do is work on me, one wound at a time. That's it. I can't do anything else in here but work on me. I can't change the past;

hell, I can't even say what I'm having for breakfast in the morning. It's not about controlling everyone else; it's not even about controlling yourself. Spirituality is about letting go of the control that you never had to begin with.

Through meditating in prison, I've learned that Christianity isn't necessarily the issue. The deeper issue is that I was a Brown kid growing up in a very White world. And in a White world, God is also White. How he acts, how he thinks, and how he perceives things is a reflection of White culture.

In my twenties, I learned that Christianity in America was not a reflection of God, but a reflection of American culture. Now in my thirties, I'm learning that Christianity in prison is not a reflection of Christianity, but a reflection of prison culture. Through my meditation, I'm learning that the divine patterns hidden underneath all the social constructs of culture aren't attached to any particular religion; the divine patterns just are. Meditation isn't Christian, Buddhist, Muslim, Jewish, Taoist, or Hindu; meditation just is. Breath isn't White, Black, or Brown. (It isn't red, white, and blue either.) Breath is breath. The key is to learn how to use it and not worry so much about how to name it.

I keep an extra set of batteries wrapped up in my pillowcase. That way people don't steal them. I pull two batteries from beneath my head and empty the dead ones out of my radio. I follow the pluses and minuses until the little red light appears on the front of my radio.

My headphones are clear and transparent. The cheap plastic is heavy and blocky. People aren't repping AirPods or

Beats headphones in prison. The red and black wires are fraying on mine, and I have to twist them so they don't unravel. Regardless, when I put my headphones on, despite the blocky uncomfortable plastic, I feel safer. I feel like I've entered a different world.

I put them on and turn the volume dial up.

The static is a cool blue in my ears.

It's a familiar feeling, like rolling the windows down when you're stuck in the backseat of the car. As I take a deep breath in, I rest the radio on my chest. I watch the radio move up and down with my breath, and I stare out at the fir trees from my window. The sun bounces off their needles and into my eyes. I exhale, and I see the needles clearly. I inhale, squint, and they blur into larger shapes. After several rounds of inhales and exhales, I decide to close my eyes and allow the familiar sun to bounce off the back of my eyelids.

The cool blue static grows louder in my ears. Before I know it, the dry fir trees are wet with the raining sound of white noise from my radio. And now, I am near them. I can touch them. There is no fence anymore, no loud inmates. It's just me, the rain, and the fir trees.

I stand underneath them looking at the bark, its patterns so intricate: fractals of brown triangles rising vertically into the sky. They root down deep into the soil and make it so there is no end or beginning. I touch the bark with my hand and feel the roughness of the tree. I walk along the row of trees brushing my hand against each trunk, feeling the different patterns of the bark. The rain grows heavy, and the needles begin to sag on the branches. Large drops of rain wet my forehead, and soon, I'm soaked to the bone. The fir trees are so quiet and majestic. They don't rage against the wind or the rain; they perfectly allow. They are gentle giants.

I can faintly feel my radio on my chest, but now I'm somewhere else. I'm engulfed in this forest of trees and rain. This meditation smells like Christmas and water. The rain is fresh and clean, and it all feels like earth. Suddenly, I see a glow behind the trees, deeper in the woods. I make my way into the forest, wending between trunks, until the glow becomes brighter.

As I turn a corner, I can see something sitting underneath the trees, a figure wrapped in light. Before I can draw closer, something erupts in the dorm, some loud noise from afar. I'm almost pulled completely from this meditation. *Stay here*, I tell myself. I quickly press my thumb to the dial on the side of the radio and crank up the volume. I won't let the prison win. The rain grows louder in the forest, and soon I'm back.

I see the glowing figure again underneath the trees, and I step closer. I am not afraid. The light is a warm light, inviting and calm. I can see now that this figure is a person, sitting cross-legged in front of the tree. A young, Brown man looks at me and smiles.

"Welcome," he says. "Do you want to sit?"

I nod and sit down across from him.

"Breathe with me," he says. As he breathes, a small gust of wind gathers strength and pushes the needles on the trees, moving the rain sideways. The trees sway back and forth mimicking the man's breath. *Is he controlling the trees?* I wonder. The man somehow can read my thoughts.

"You wonder if my breath is guiding the trees, but perhaps the trees are guiding my breath."

"Who are you?" I ask.

"Who do you want me to be?" I get the feeling that he's some holy man, maybe a historical figure, but I'm not sure.

"Are you Jesus? Buddha? I don't know... a stranger?" I ask.

"Yes, if that helps," replies the man.

"Yes, to which? Jesus or Buddha?"

"Why do they have to be different?" the stranger answers.

"I don't follow," I respond.

"Tell me, who was Jesus before Jesus?"

"To be honest, I don't really care."

"Yes," the man says calmly. "That is fair. I can see your skin is hot. It boils with anger." As he says it, I can feel my teeth begin to clench. I can feel my body posturing defensively.

But then I hear a familiar voice.

Breathe.

As I watch the man's demeanor, I feel my heart begin to slow down. I take a deep breath in and try to relax my muscles. After all, I know this is just a meditation, and I'm somewhere deep in my own body.

"Is that rain?" the man asks me, looking up at the falling drops.

"No, it's just the static from my radio," I reply.

"Ah, I see." the man says, still smiling. "Please, please, tell me. Why is your skin so hot?"

"I guess, it's hot because I don't know if I want to be here."

"With me?" asks the man.

"I don't really want to have a conversation with Jesus. I'm just not into that anymore."

The stranger chuckles a bit and softens his hands.

"Perhaps, it's best that I am not Jesus then."

"I don't understand. Can you choose who you are?" I ask puzzled.

"If things could be so easy," the man laughs. "You are somewhere else, yes? Not really here in this forest, yes?"

I nod in response.

"But how are you so sure you aren't here?" he continues. "Why is meditation less real than the prison you are a part of up there?"

I shake my head.

"I don't know," I answer.

"If we are just in your body, then why are our identities separate? And if they are not separate, then can't we be whoever it is we are? Can I not be Jesus and can I not also be Buddha? Can I not also just be you?"

"I'm not sure I'm looking for riddles."

"This is not a riddle. It's quite simple, really. We humans like to see things separately. It makes it easier for us to see a tree when we look at a tree. But perhaps we need to look closer? When the divine speaks, maybe the divine is showing up as the thing you are seeing, but it is not just the thing you are seeing. There is always something underneath the thing."

"Right," I respond. "Energy is energy is energy."

"Exactly," replies the stranger. "You have clothes. Underneath those clothes, you have skin, muscles, blood, and bones. And underneath those bones, molecules and atoms, and underneath those atoms... they have a name for it now."

"Quarks," I respond.

"Yes, yes. Quarks. And these quarks, they are in you, yes? And they are in these trees? Maybe this Jesus you don't like very much — maybe these quarks were in him too. Perhaps it was the energy within him that was speaking all along. Perhaps the man was not so much the point, but the energy underneath. So again, I ask you... why is your skin so hot?"

"Maybe because I'm surrounded by assholes all the damn time. Meditating is exhausting; living in prison is exhausting."

"Well, it certainly isn't the Holiday Inn. But if I may…again, where is God?"

"God?" I reply. "I'm not sure I really care, to be honest."

"Okay, you don't like that term, replace it with another one. Life. Energy. Universe. Love. Source. Where is it? Is it in this tree? Is it in the mountain? Is it in the birds?"

"Sure, I get what you're saying…yes. The Universe is in those things."

"No. You need to look. Look at the tree."
I look over at the fir tree, and to my surprise, what was once rough edges of brown bark, has now been replaced with a glowing light, the same light from the man.

"Look closer," I hear him say to me.

As I look closer, I notice that these lights are the same lights I've seen my whole life, glowing and dancing and bouncing radiantly off of each other. The hot pinks and blues, greens and reds, are exploding, rising and falling up and down the trunk of the tree.

"You can touch the tree. You are safe."

I reach over to touch the tree, and immediately, the lights begin to flow up my arm. In moments, my arm is no longer my arm, but a sea of these same lights. I can still make out the outline of my arm, but it is no longer skin and flesh, bone and muscle; it's just lights. I can't make out where the tree ends and my arm begins, but somehow, I am not scared. This is not a suffocating feeling; this is a welcoming one. The light travels up my arm and begins to flow through my shoulders and my back. I look over at the man. He is smiling.

"Perhaps, what you see here in this meditation is more a reality than what you see up there in the prison. Perhaps, what is in the tree is also in you, no?"

"The things that I look for out there, I can find in myself, right?" I ask the man.

"If you can see it here, you can see it anywhere. If you see it in the trees, you can see it in the mountains, no? So, if I am Jesus, perhaps I am not just a Jesus. Perhaps, I am a you or a mountain or a tree or a buddha. Split a piece of wood, I am there. Lift up a stone, I am there too. And so are you. And so are those angry men that you live with. This Jesus man is not so important. If he gets in the way, then let him go. If something keeps you from discovering the gentle flow underneath, then perhaps it is not necessary for you to hold on to? Don't let your skin boil so hot. If you can remove the thing that makes you boil, then that is a good thing."

"You're saying… I don't have to believe in anything if I don't want to?"

"Perhaps I am saying, if it no longer gives you life, then let it go. Then the thing that gives you life will come to you. If it helps to see it in a tree, then see it in a tree. If it helps to see it in a river, then see it in a river. And if it helps to see it in a Jesus, then see it in a Jesus. One day, you will see that even the harshest things are still included."

"Harshest? Like, the racist inmates? And homophobic Christians?" I ask.

"Yes, them."

"And the White supremacists?"

"Them too."

"What if I don't want to see it in them?"

"Then you do not have to. It means it is not time for you to see it in them. Let go of what hurts, that is the quickest way to heal. If you hold onto what hurts you, then how can you expect to heal? The energies are energies of mercy. They do not require anything of you. That is what makes them merciful. No matter what the case is, you belong."

"There are no requirements?"

"None," the stranger says with a smile. "That is the real secret. You already belong, even before your birth, you have belonged."

"That is hard for me to process."

"Don't process. There is no need. The key is to drop out of the mind and drop into the body. The body is what allows you to see; the mind is what keeps you from seeing. Stop trying to see with your head, my friend."

"Okay, so now what?" I ask.

"Now, we listen to the rain."

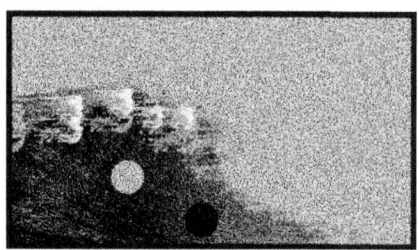

Meditation

Dear friends,

What guides you?
Is it your imagination? Your creativity?
Is it the desire to dream, to have, to grow, to be?
Is it something physical or spiritual or both? Is it something outside you or something within?

Lights and colors have been the way the Universe has manifested physically in my life, to help me navigate the labyrinth of my own shadow (as well as the complex duality of the American prison system). But I imagine, like the flow of creativity itself, the Universe will show up differently for you than it did for me. We are all unique little flowers in a large meadow — a meadow that makes up all things. When you look closely, you see that every flower, though unique in its own way, is made up of the same thing underneath — a Universe within, and a Universe without. So, do not be so worried, dear friends, if the Universe shows up differently for you than for your neighbor. It is still the same Universe showing up.

Becoming nature

We can begin to find patterns within us that can help point us to how the Divine shows up for us individually. Nature has always been a good grounding place for me in my life. If you have access to a field, a forest, some place in the trees, an ocean, or a river, you are already ten steps ahead of where I was when I began my meditation journey through prison. Of course, my lack of access to nature was probably what compelled my meditations to manifest as creatively as they did.

In other words, sometimes having less access to the natural manifestations of the Universe (oceans, trees, rivers, mountains, stars, etc.) causes the source deep within us to manifest more forcefully. The magnitude of such energy held and then stirred within the body directly affects the levels of imagination within our own spirit.

I would be doing the Universe a large injustice if I did not say first: Nature will always be a much better teacher than myself. So, immerse yourself in it. Go for a hike, get on the water, go kayaking, or swimming in a lake. Become a part of it. When I sit by the ocean, I become the ocean. Become a part of the land that encapsulates you.

Discovering nature outside of you shows you the nature within you.

Your body is an ocean, alive and flowing and full of unimaginable depth. A wave within and a wave without. Your body is a tree, resilient and grounded, alive and full of hope. It is important to spend time around energy much larger than us; it grounds us and reminds us that we are a part of something greater and more eternal than the fragile ego identity we constantly cling to.

We can learn from the trees, just as we can learn from the light. It's all about how we choose to see, not about what we see.

A meditative exercise in nature

Be outside. Find a place under a tree, by a river, lake, or mountain — some place calm. First, start by just sitting and allowing the sun, rain, or overcast sky to fill you up. Just sit with it. Imagine that the air is like water. Imagine that the light is like water, that it can drench you to your bone. Just sit for a moment.

You are no different from the tree that shades you.

Close your eyes and feel part of the nature that you've chosen to surrender to. If you are sitting near a lake, feel the water; if you are sitting by a river, dip your hand in its current; if you are sitting under a tree, feel its bark; if you are sitting on a mountain, put your hand in the snow.

What does it feel like? With your eyes closed, describe it to yourself through feeling.
The goal is to get out of the thinking mind again and into the feeling body. You have to learn through feeling.

Our ego tricks us into thinking that because this thing feels or looks like something different than us, then it must be something wholly other. The ego likes to distinguish and create a hierarchy, always putting itself at the top. Like the parts within your own body, I encourage you to begin to create relationships with these different parts of the earth: create a dialogue between you and the water, between you and the current, between you and the bark, between you and the snow. After creating the relationship, it is always easier to see what you have in common instead of what you don't. In meditation, this is key: connection, not separation.

When you ask the land to become a part of you, you are opening yourself up to the possibility that you are not at the center of existence. This aperture begins your journey of letting go of what was. Perhaps, without knowing it, you are inviting a wisdom energy that heals through the allowing of suffering, instead of its avoidance. This is the wisdom of the earth: she always allows because she knows that life arrives only after death. Trees allow the falling of leaves, the burning of forests, and the lighting of fires, knowing that new growth will form. The ocean experiences the diurnal tides, the ebb and flow, the Dao of rising and falling. The earth instinctually welcomes death and newness through her seasons. Simply sitting and becoming aware of this deeper pattern in all things prepares us spiritually to readily accept our own rising and falling and rising again.

Are you ready, dear friends?

Afterall, we cannot die without dying.

Before Enlightenment, a mountain is a mountain.
During enlightenment, a mountain is not a mountain.
After enlightenment, a mountain is a mountain.

Chapter Six

Reiki in the Snow

The snow feels colder in prison. I think because everything is metal here. All the weights are out in the yard, and each weight is connected to heavy chains. Sometimes the chains are heavier than the weights themselves. The dumbbells are connected to the chains so that inmates can't take them away and beat someone with them. It's true.

I never lifted weights before prison, not like this. I am dedicated in here. My body uses all my pent-up adrenaline and cortisol on exercising and working out. When I raise the weights up above my head, I can hear the chains sloshing on the wet snow, clanging together like dull wind chimes. The metal freezes my hands. By the end of my workout, my palms are throbbing in the cold. I can smell the iron out here. Even with the snow, the air is not fresh; it reeks of tobacco and dried blood.

Sometimes when it snows here, the guards don't let you outside at all. We're trapped like tigers. Winter freezes everything, and it makes time slower than it already is, which makes everyone more eager to get out on the yard. People who can afford boots wear boots, and others willingly martyr their feet just to get some time off of their bunks. Men hide contraband in their off-brand sneakers, and they use yard time to form their own personal stock exchange. People roll joints and doobies around the aglet of their laces, just to sneak them past the guards. I watch the hustle take place from afar. They trade coffee for cigarettes, and ice cream for weed. The higher-priced items, they trade for big bags. Honestly, even now, I'm not quite sure what constitutes a big bag (other than the amount of money that goes into it).

Some men stomp their feet or give hand signals for when they want to trade something, that way the guards can't catch them talking. Sign language and signals are an integral part of prison culture. The inmates get paid at the first of the month. It's the same thing every time. It doesn't matter if it's March 1 or December 1; if it's the first, you know there's going to be a whole lot of stomping and hand signaling.

The inmates who are newer to prison are called fishes, so they have less money on their books (money in their commissary accounts). The fishes have to resort to wearing cheap, generic, off-brand Converse, that the inmates call CONS, for obvious reasons. Their shoes are flimsy and feel like cardboard. Even the smell of rain gets them wet — a poor choice in Oregon. You can always tell who's a new fish in here; they're the ones with drenched feet.

Thankfully, I have boots, so it's easier for me to weather the Oregon puddles. Often, I stand off to the side near the outer fence, and I watch the fishes wander the yard in their CONS, desperately trying to figure out how to get in with the right car.

When it's cold, I bundle up with all the clothes I have, but all my clothes are baggy and caked in denim. They don't tailor clothes for people my size, so I constantly find myself rolling my sleeves up like a kindergartner. My jean jacket hangs past my knees. It's such a stupid idea to issue jean jackets in a place like this. Denim never does well in the snow or the rain.

I spend my time lifting weights until the pile gets too crowded with men. Crowds invite impatience, and impatience invites fights. Anger, testosterone, and lack of self-control is not a good recipe for healing work. Listening to the body in a place like this is key. Somehow my body knows exactly when it's time to leave. I can tell when things are heating up. My body warns me like a lighthouse, letting me know when the ships are getting too close to the cliffs. It's happened so many times, I've lost count, but it always starts the same way:

I'm lifting weights by myself, and then I hear the noise of men bickering behind me. It's the same argument every time. Most men don't have the wherewithal to listen to anyone else but their own ego. (It's why nothing ever gets done in Congress — too many men, too many egos.) Sometimes I picture politicians here, lifting dumbbells, weighted down by chains. I picture their inner fragility exposed to the cold snow and metal. I wonder what kind of argument they could make in a place like this.

The aggression burgeons quickly. At first, it's all tongue, then it's fists. You can tell things are picking up by the way the weights bang against the benches. I can feel it in my bones, the same way you feel it when you know you've left the burner on or the garage door open. I feel it in my legs and on the back of my neck.

You're no longer safe. It's time to put the weights down and leave.

It's a hard thing to do when you just started your work out, you only have three more reps to go, or you know it's your only yard time because the guards are too cold. But I'd rather be three reps short than get pummeled for being in the wrong place at the wrong time.

I've seen more fights than I can count. They call it

gladiator school. The fights are always based on something so small and stupid, like someone changing the channel of the TV in the day room or grabbing a book on the shelf that someone had planned to read themselves. Why does it matter so much? All the pages are torn out anyway. Out on the yard, fights often happen when two men go for the same weight. The smell of blood doesn't wash out well, and against the weight and iron, it's enough to make anyone feel a little queasy after seeing two young kids go at it. Though there are plenty of fights inside, the yard is usually the place to handle business. I've learned that if someone takes your weight, you let them. Here you own nothing, and it's better that way.

I walk the track in the snow. I can see my boot prints in the white. The dirt mixes in with the falling snow, and the mud underneath creates a sludge sound under my heels. The snow is crisp today, crisp and powdery, and when I walk, it sounds like the crunching of leaves. The snow is peaceful and calms my body like lavender. The track is farther away from the weight pile, so it's less noisy but still busy. There's no solitude in a place like this; you're never alone. Like everything else, I mind my own business and keep my head down. I hide my cold ears underneath my blue beanie, and I rub my hands together to create heat. The crunch of the snow and the rubbing of my hands begins to create a rhythm. I can hear the sound of my hands rubbing together, and I try to line it up with the crunch of each heel. After I've created a rhythm, I try to align my inhales and exhales too. Left foot down, crunch of snow, slide hand up, inhale. Right foot down, crunch of snow, slide hand down, exhale. Repeat.

Meditation is all about finding a rhythm, and it always starts with a physical one. It's why prayer beads can be found in every religion. Men and women have used prayer beads for thousands of years. Rubbing your thumbs against the beads creates a rhythm too. When you repeat a mantra with your voice paired with the physical action of sliding the beads through your thumbs, it gets you into a deeper rhythm of the earth. Sometimes I do the same with the volume dial on my radio; it has the same effect. The deeper rhythms are always there for us, but it's often we who don't really know how to enter into them. Participating in the deeper rhythm creates a different kind of frequency in you. It's the same reason why drum circles can be so powerful. Like Wu Wei, you are entering into a larger river.

As I walk around the track, I'm intentional about each step. I try to notice how my knees feel when they bend and how my ankles feel when they hit the loose rocks. Everything is connected in the body. Every tendon connects to another. Muscles wrap around bones and fascia. In traditional Chinese medicine (TCM), meridians connect to the acupuncture points and fascia. Each meridian connects to different organ systems. The twelve meridians are separated into yin and yang: lung, heart, pericardium, kidney, liver, spleen (yin) and large and small intestines, triple burner (upper, lower and middle torso), stomach, bladder, and gall bladder (yang).

It's all connected, and it starts with just listening to your body and feeling each part. When my calves are tight, I can feel it in my lower back. Pretty soon the pain is in my shoulders and my neck. I'm not an acupuncturist, and I know very little about TCM, but I try to feel the meridians within my body. Though not physical anatomical structures and not recognized in Western medicine, meridians carry the Chi energy from one part of the body to another.

I picture the energy running up from my heel to my hips. I breathe in, left foot down, crunch of snow, slide of hand up. I invite the chi, and I surrender to it. Exhale, right foot down, crunch of snow, slide hand down. It feels warm in my cold body in the same way hot chocolate feels on its first gulp. I'm not sure how to name it, but I'm also not sure if that's important. Breath is breath.

I'm a Reiki Master (still not a term I completely agree with). I've learned to sense the energy. Reiki isn't about control, which is why I don't think the word "master" is fitting. In America, "master" has too many racial connotations, and in Reiki, you aren't really mastering anything anyway. The idea is that the Reiki energy goes where it goes. As the Reiki Master, you are just a conduit to help it get there. Through my Reiki practice, I've learned to understand how energy works; it takes a lifetime of practice, but I'm a lifelong learner. I can feel the different energy parts in my body as I walk in the snow. I can sense when the energy is trapped or blocked, and I can also sense when it's surging fast.

In Reiki healing, you have sacred symbols that represent spiritual gateways for the Reiki energy to enter your body. The Cho Ku Rei is a symbol of power, but not in the way we think about power and certainly not in the way people in prison think about power.

The Cho Ku Rei is sacred symbol for the power of the Universe, right here, and right now. Most importantly, the Cho Ku Rei is an invitation to surrender to that power. I've learned in my practice to always draw the symbol somewhere on my body with my finger, just before repeating the mantra. I do this often when I walk the yard. Drawing the symbol becomes a mantra in itself, like the sign of the cross in the Christian tradition. The Cho Ku Rei symbol looks like the number seven entering into a spiral. I cannot help but sense the deeper meaning of Cho Ku Rei, especially in a place like prison where there is nowhere to go; Prison is an endless spiral too. My meditation practice teaches me that the spiritual spiral isn't one that spirals up toward heaven, but a spiraling inward — into the body. Somehow, this symbol works perfectly.

When I walk the track, I envision this spiritual spiral before me, every lap moving inward, further and further into my own body. The snow falls heavy but not enough to compromise visibility for the guards. Nobody wants a strong snow in here. When that happens, we're all forced to go back to our bunks. The snow further underscores that I am just a small Brown body in a sea of White (as if I need reminding). For the most part, walking the track is peaceful, but occasionally, there are moments of disruption.

I walk the track clockwise. Though I walk in one direction, I'm always aware of my surroundings, of those running past me and those running behind me. I keep my head down and my intention focused on the Reiki. I can hear someone coming up behind me. They're running, so I'm safe. (It's the fast walkers you've got to worry about.) I can hear the footsteps gathering speed behind me. I look back and then down at his feet. He's not wearing CONS, so that's a good sign. Usually, the ones who call the shots have the fish run their errands for them, like throwing punches, or worse. The fact that he has running shoes on means he's probably just doing that — running.

But as he runs by me, he shoves me hard with his elbow.

"Out of my way, Muhammed."

I try to ignore the extremity of his belligerence. I try to breathe, but I immediately get angry. There's so much that I could say, but I stay quiet. I'm not sure how those who practiced nonviolent resistance, the Gandhis or the MLKs, could do it so well for so long. More often than not, I'd rather throw the chair than sit in it.

When I get called those names, it takes all the strength in me not to react. I can tell a part of me goes somewhere else in my body, like I'm hiding from a part of my past that I have yet to face. It took me months and months of calming the mind to see past my initial blinding reaction. When you're called something derogatory and dehumanizing, your whole body naturally tenses up. The defense is instantaneous. The fawning side of my youth wants to jump out of my skin and say something witty back, but it's just not worth it. In a game of punching babies, there are no winners, I think humorously to myself. I'd like to say that the reactions within me have gotten better, but I'm human. Sometimes it's the small things that boil a person.

The familiar voice always comes to me when I need it. *Hold onto your Reiki. Don't let him win.*

I breathe in deep, and the freezing air fills my lung. It's sharp, and it feels as though I'm catching my first breath of life. When you let the anger go, it doesn't always fade quickly; more often than not, the anger lingers like a cough. Yet, the bite of the snow freezes this anger all the way out. In minutes, I've almost already forgotten what he said. I can feel the Cho Ku Rei supporting me.

I breathe in and invite the Reiki. I invite the snow. I invite my breath. I'm reminded of Wim Hof in this moment. I'm reminded of his primal outlook on the body. The breath really does separate us. It separates the alive, from the barely alive. I take a huge Wim Hof breath in, and let the exhalation fill the sky as I draw the Cho Ku Rei symbol across my chest with my cold fingers.

Reiki, I invite you, I say. Please meet me here so that I can listen. When it comes, it hits me like a prizefighter. Immediately, I feel the rush of energy surge throughout my body. Somehow the snow enhances the warmth within my own body. I try to stay present as I breathe deep, still paying attention to the crunching rhythm of my heels in the snow.

I don't have my radio, but I don't need it outside. The falling snow is my gateway. The Reiki is my white noise. I close my eyes as I walk, only opening them every few moments to see where I am going. Each time I close my eyes, I see the snow grow whiter in my mind. Soon, everything is a blizzard, and I'm no longer in this yard, on this track, walking this endless loop. Now the snow has transported me, and I'm on the brae of a mountainside somewhere. The snow is deep, and I'm up past my waist but not cold. I try to take a step forward, but I fall deeper into the frost. Now, I'm up to my shoulders, but I'm breathing; I'm still not worried. Something inside me is telling me to sludge forward. I take another step and fall deeper, the snow past my neck. Suddenly, I feel the snow beneath my feet give away, and I sink beneath the surface of the mountainside. Falling deeper and deeper, I can feel myself tunneling down into the cold white.

Moments later, I am cocooned in a sea of snow, and though it's cold, it's liberating. Normally, I'm claustrophobic. I hate elevators, closets, and crowds, but somehow, I don't feel panicked here. Maybe it's because I know this is a meditation, and somewhere up there, I am still walking loops around the track of the prison. Nevertheless, my breath has led me here, so here is where I am.

Though I'm completely caved in, I find myself in an artificial air pocket. There's a little wiggle room to move my hands and feet. The air pocket has changed the oxygen levels. Every breath feels like 100 breaths. My eyes are open and clear, and my lungs are full. When I breathe in, I breathe in for minutes at a time. The breath makes me feel more alive.

I look down at my feet and notice something dark just below my boots. I adjust my arms, pushing them down around my side, to grab what's at my feet. I reach down and grab what feels like a small pebble, but when I bring it up back up into view, I notice it's not a rock but a seed.

When I first got to prison everybody noticed me. I was this small little Brown thing, surrounded by large, angry, muscular White men. I wasn't a threat, and yet somehow, I was. Of course, not physically, but for some reason people seemed to be irritated just by looking at me. My state-issued clothes were so baggy that I looked like a kid. I think that made a bit of a difference. Before I learned the laws, I didn't have much to offer people in prison. Everything is bartered, and everything is about what you can trade or market to another. The gifts that I have are very useful on the outside, but not in a place like this. Prison is an upside-down world. It plays by its own rules, and it's up to you figure them out, because no one is going to take the time to teach you.

People called me camel, sand nigger, Muhammed, or some other Middle-Eastern racist slur when I got to prison. The funny thing is no one ever asked about me, not once. Nobody cares because if someone is hurting you, it means that someone is not hurting them. Everybody assumed I was Muslim and that I couldn't speak English very well. I have heard far too many "America" grunts, enough to last several lifetimes. (Honestly, even one "America" grunt is one too many.) Ironically, I'm probably one of the very few people in here who have exercised their constitutional right to vote. Doesn't that make me more American?

My Brownness seemed to irritate people in ways that I hadn't experienced before. I could tell that people were put off just by looking at me. It's a strange feeling having everybody look at you that way, yet at the same time, it's a feeling I think I've known my whole life. I don't think I could piece the puzzle together when I was younger, but the puzzle pieces make perfect sense here.

I had always thought it to be a pretty superficial stereotype, but it's true: If you have Brown skin, people think you're dirty, literally dirty. I had one neighbor next to me that assumed I was gay because I was Brown. (Not that being gay makes you bad or dirty, but that is the assumption amongst many of the White men here.) When I asked my neighbor why he thought all Brown people were gay, he looked at me straight-faced and said, "Brown people are faggots. That's just what I was taught." He told me that's what he learned from his parents. When you look deep enough, you begin to see that the patterns go miles and miles into our pasts. It didn't start with these men; it didn't even start with their parents or their parents' parents.

This seed looks so strange in my hand. I'm covered in snow, but this seed looks fresh, as if it's a sign of spring. The snow is silent, and the silence brings a stillness that I am not used to in prison. The stillness of the snow is purifying in a way that other things aren't. In the snow, our breaths are active and full, like smoke rising from a flame. As I look down at the seed, I have a strange flash of memory come to the forefront of my mind: a ten-year-old me, frozen on the edge of a glacier.

It's a memory of me camping at the basin of a high lake in the Eagle Cap mountains of eastern Oregon. I remember everything was blanketed in snow. My family and I had gone backpacking for a week up in the mountains. I was young, and everything was an adventure. We brought tents and water purifiers; we built fires and ate freeze-dried food. We had eggs for breakfast and jerky for lunch. It was early summer, and we expected some snow. But when we reached camp five miles in from the trailhead, we quickly discovered that winter was far from over.

We set up camp near the lake so we could collect water when we needed a drink or wanted to cook. Since it was summer, my family had packed a small inflatable raft; we assumed we'd want to swim and be in the water. (How we were able to pack in a raft is beyond me.) In the middle of the lake was a small glacier, still frozen and packed with snow from the winter months prior. Being the little adventurers that we were, my brother and I were determined to get to the middle of the lake and stand on top of the glacier like two little Indian Edmund Hillarys.

We paddled out in our small raft with a single plastic oar for what felt like hours of paddling but was probably only fifteen minutes. When we reached the iceberg, it was a lot bigger than we thought. My brother got out of the raft first and helped pull me up. I hadn't thought to wear sandals or shoes, so I was barefoot. My feet were already wet from the lake, and when I stepped onto the glacier, I could feel my feet freeze instantly. The vapor rising from the glacier into the summer air looked like smoke around my ankles. My brother, who had been smart enough to wear shoes, pranced around the glacier, jumping up and down trying to break off a chunk of ice to take back to the camp with us.

"It's a good way to keep the beer cold," I remember him saying.

"You're eleven," I responded back.

As my brother got to work breaking off chunks of the iceberg, I remember just staring at my feet, at the vapor rising. I remember feeling so cold but so alive. As I looked out at the lake from our conquest, I couldn't help but feel a part of something, something much larger than myself. I distinctly remember looking up at the peak of the small mountain above the lake and noticing a part of the peak where it broke off from the rest of the mountainside. The part that lifted up in the air looked like an arm raising its fist up into the sky. There were pockets of snow missing from the rising rock, and the shape of the arm made it look like little dark spots up and down the column of the mountain. As I looked down at the rest of the lake, I noticed that my arms were starting to stiffen from the cold. The little hairs began to rise on my arm as goosebumps appeared.

I watched the goosebumps appear on my arm in real time. Where do these things come from? At one moment, they're nowhere, and the next moment, they're everywhere. I lifted my cold arm up into the air to try and warm it in the summer sun. As I lifted it, I noticed the strangest thing — my arm, my gangly little Indian arm, looked exactly like the column on the mountain rising into the sky. And even more so, I noticed the goosebumps that had formed on my arm looked like the spots on the mountain where the snow was missing. It was too much of a coincidence for my ten-year-old mind to fathom. I looked down at my frozen arm, back up at the mountain, and then back down at my arm again. I couldn't help but notice the patterns were exactly the same — the snow, the goosebumps, the cold on my arm, the way it rose up into the sky exactly the way the mountain did. I watched the vapor rising from the glacier beneath my feet like smoke and couldn't help but notice that it looked the same as the smoke-vapor rising from the tip of the mountain peak, glistening in the sun. I am the mountain, and the mountain is me. I am a Brown speck of a kid, in a sea of white snow and ice, yet this mountain and I are the same.

I'm still in this air pocket of snow, deep in meditation. I know that I'm walking around the track still, somewhere up there, but not right now. Here, down in this peaceful state, I am surrounded by snow and ice. I look down at the brown seed in my hand. It's a smaller version of my backpacking memory — a small brown seed in a sea of white snow. Everything is connected. We are not separate. The memory isn't a distant one; it's right here, right next to me in this seed.

In the quiet moment of understanding, I hear a voice. *Nelumbo.*

Honestly, I have no idea what Nelumbo means. I don't think I've even heard the word before.

Have I?

I must have, because I'm deep in my own meditation, in my own body, in my own subconscious. How could I possibly hear a word that I haven't heard of before?

Nelumbo, the voice says again. *Peel it.*

The snow begins to melt around me, turning into an ocean of water. I begin to float softly, holding the seed in my hand.

I gently place my thumbs on the seed and start to pull the shell apart. It starts to crack like an egg. Inside the brown shell is a white casing. Suddenly, a sprout begins to form from inside the seed. The green sprout begins to twist its way up out of the seed like a snake, growing larger and larger in seconds. It bursts out of the brown shell, cracking it in half, exploding up out of the water and snow. I grab onto the stalk with both my hands as it carries me upward to the surface of the mountain that I had once fallen from.

The stalk breaks the surface of the snow forcefully, carrying me with it. I jump off the stalk onto the ice. Leaves begin to form around the top of the sprout; they look like lily pads. Everything is growing fast around me, and I feel like I'm in a time lapse video. The sprout is growing so quickly, but I'm standing still. Multiple sprouts now erupt from below the surface where the seed had been, all rising out of the earth in columns of vines. At the end of the leaves are flowers, but I can't see them yet. They are still enclosed, waiting to bloom.

Pink and purple petals quickly begin to manifest from their enclosed leaves. I notice there is a tint of yellow closer to the center of the flower. I recognize the flowers immediately — they are lotuses.

The ancient flower has been a sign of resilience and spiritual purity for centuries. Distinctly known for their ability to blossom in the dirt and the mud, the lotus is a symbol of hope and being reborn out of hurt. It is a constant symbol of awakening to something new and everlasting. A brown seed in a sea of white bursting forth into a lotus flower out of the earth; it's no coincidence.

But like an alarm clock disrupting someone from the safety of their peaceful dreams, I hear a buzzing sound blaring across the mountain, though it's not coming from the mountain. It's coming from the security towers of the prison. I suddenly break awake and out of my meditation. I'm still pacing around the track. The alarm buzzes from the prison PA, signaling the end of my yard time.

I heard my professor from college once tell me,

"Before enlightenment a mountain is a mountain, during enlightenment a mountain is not a mountain, and after enlightenment a mountain is a mountain."

We are all on a journey to try and figure out what this whole thing is — life. We are all trying figure out where we went wrong, if we went wrong, and how we fit into this larger thing. We are all just small specks staring up at massive mountains, but when we look close enough, we begin to see that the mountains look like us. It's somehow all connected; the patterns are the same everywhere. The same mathematical ratios that make up the spirals in our galaxies, also known as the golden ratio (1.618), make up the spirals in a seashell. The Fibonacci sequence in a wave on the ocean can be found in the patterns of a pinecone. From succulents to the double-helix within our own DNA, the patterns are waiting for us. We are invited to awaken to the reality of which we are a part.

Though I'm here in this prison — a Brown-skinned person in a sea of White supremacists and Nazi sympathizers — I'm somehow a part of the whole. I'm a part of the fabric that makes up the entire blanket. As I make my way around the track and back into the dorm, I wonder: is this thing we call God in the snowflakes that fall, the distant ocean, or the mountains beyond the ridge? Is God in the clouds, the birds, and the deer? Is God in my dog at home or my parents' horses? How could God not be?

Though I am not Christian or White, I wonder, is their White Christian God in me too? Though I imagine most of them would say no, I can't help but believe even their God is in me, somehow. The Reiki reminds me that when I look at my arms, at the stupid little goosebumps I get when it's too cold because I don't have enough blankets on my bunk, somehow, God is in those goosebumps too. Somehow, I am included in the best way possible. I am the mountain, and the mountain is me.

Meditation

Dear friends,

There is something about the cold: the rawness and austerity eat at all of me.

Its biting sting always seems to remind me of exactly where I am. More often than not, it's the last thing I want to be reminded of.

Like the agonizing feeling of numb fingers on frozen metal, the Universe can sometimes seem unkind in her approach to reaching you. I assure you, dear friends, if we zoom out and pause just for a bit, we'll start to see there's a hidden kindness underneath.

Reiki energy teaches me to slow down. Yet, in my experience, being in the cold makes me want to speed everything else up. This juxtaposition makes meditating outside in the cold a perfect place to be. It is the spiritual brilliance of opposition, holding the "both/and" together in the present moment.

I can only speak to my experience, but Reiki energizes me, less like a raging fire and more like a slurp from of a warm cup of soup. In her warmth, I am still reminded of the cold. When we slow down each breath and each movement, we become more appreciative of every passing moment. We become still, and then we become aware.

When I meditate, the anger comes first. It's natural to want to react to what comes first instead of waiting patiently for what may come after. Meditating in the cold, however, gets to the feeling underneath the anger, bringing the one question to the surface that we'd rather have stay buried:

Are you sure there isn't something else going on?

Like the roots of a tree spreading out into deep soil or a small seed hidden in the heart of a mountain, the wound often isn't where we think it is. The cold can challenge us to go there.

The cold brings an honesty to meditation, and the Reiki compels me to trust that such honesty will always lead me to places inside myself that I have yet to journey. The key is to actually lean into it. It is natural to think that the best way to meditate and imagine is to close your eyes and pretend you are somewhere else. The opposite is actually true.

Part of learning to meditate deeply and visualize creatively is actually to stay in the body and stay in the moment, not escape it or deflect from it. The body will naturally lead you to where it is you need to go. The cold is a wonderful way to be present to what is.

A showering pain

Cold immersion is a great way to learn about the presence of pain. In my experience of being out in nature, a cold lake, or river can lead you right into it. Like my young self standing barefoot on a glacier out in the middle of the lake in the Eagle Cap mountains, the cold has a way of connecting us to the deeper movement of presence. Standing barefoot in winter in the snow or frozen grass has a way of connecting us to the Earth. Every day during my meditation time, I try to stand outside barefoot, rain or shine, in gratitude. This is one way I stay connected. This is one way I stay present.

Cold showers can also lead you right into it; being immersed in cold water teaches you to be honest with yourself in ways that you otherwise may not be. Like a surge of lightning, cold showers can remind you instantaneously what you are afraid of or what you've been avoiding. I've jumped into a cold shower or a freezing lake and have been surprised by what came up in my body. It shows you things you've been holding onto, often things you didn't even know were there.

It is important to breathe deeply before taking a cold shower or immersing in cold water. Deep breaths are a good way to prepare your body, as well as your spirit, to go into the water. The cold water is truly a cleansing ritual, not to be taken lightly. The pain of the cold shower feels like icy daggers. It will cause you to do everything you think you need to do to get out. In other words, it can stimulate a fight or flight response. As in all meditation exercises, be gentle with yourself. (You know your body much better than I do. I am not a doctor. If you feel like you might have any underlying conditions in your body that could be affected by cold water, please consult with your doctor first.) It is important to go into the cold like you would into any other meditation: with an open energy of love and not of fear. The cold is not a punishment, nor should it be seen as one. The cold is just a tool that can teach us how to allow what is.

Before stepping into the cold shower, I meditate. I suggest you sit with your body for five to ten minutes, focusing on your breath. Taking deep breaths, breathe into your belly, pause for five seconds, and then breathe up from your gut and out through your mouth. Go with the rhythm of your breath and with the rhythm of your body; do not force it. After ten minutes of breathing, turn on the shower and invite the cold to teach you. Inviting the cold and inviting the Universe to participate with you will give you a little more trust for what may open up within you. I suggest starting with thirty seconds, and, over time, working up to two minutes and then to five minutes.

At first, your whole body will resist it.

You will want to get out.

This is normal.

Breathe into it.

Breathe with it.

If you stay with it long enough, you will hear a voice within you. This voice will say something like:

Allow it.

or

Just be with it.

Trust that voice; it is your deepest self pulling you inward. This is surrender.

Being in the cold will put you right where you are. It is only in this moment that you can begin to learn about the hidden parts of yourself that lay dormant. We must all go down into that deep, dark shadow within and discover ourselves in new ways. Before we can go to our younger parts, we must first know where to look. Cold and meditation can teach us to pause long enough to be present so we can see where we must go. Listen for the voice between your breaths. This voice will instinctually guide you into the deeper waters of your own heart.

Chapter Seven

A Lid on the Jar

Sometimes I feel like I am trapped in my body.

Sometimes I feel like I am only my body.

I know this isn't true, because when I close my eyes, I go somewhere else, away from this place. Yet, I still exist. I still am. My breath grounds me. My breath reminds me of where I am. I am not past or future, but only here. The paradox of meditating in the body is that the more grounded I feel, the more I become greater than just the body I inhabit. This Brown body is a gateway. It determines how I see everything else. That is, it makes all things small and all things powerful at the same time.

When I am present to every cell in my body — every pain, every muscle, every bone, and every joint — I become more connected to everything else outside my body. The joy I feel in my body is the joy a person feels halfway across the world. In meditation, I feel that joy. The pain I feel in this place is the same pain people incarcerated felt hundreds of years ago. I feel that pain in meditation too. Suffering is around me all the time, but so is joy. Right now, the two are hidden in plain sight, disguised in the form of my incarceration.

I can feel my muscles in my jaw begin to loosen. With every inhale and every exhale, my body releases the tension that prison brings. I feel it often in my lower back. That is where I hold my pain. That is where I hold my trauma. I can feel an energy the size of a tennis ball stuck down at the base of my spine. I get angry because I can feel myself pushing against it, and no matter how hard I push, I can't seem to release it. When I breathe in through my nostrils and out through my mouth, I notice it in a new way. I allow it to be. I no longer try and push it out. The energy is still there, but I'm no longer pushing against it. Sometimes I put my hands on my lower back to try to relieve the pain. I can feel it pulsing. I can feel a light held there; it feels organic, from the earth or even deeper. It feels like it's coming from a place I have yet to discover, and yet, a place I've always been.

The radio in my hand is plastic, man-made, and material, but it also feels a part of me now, too. The plastic is see-through, which gives it an even cheaper quality. It feels like a toy you get in a Happy Meal. I can see the green circuit board inside with all the little resistors, inductors, transformers, and diodes. The radios are transparent because the prison doesn't want you hiding contraband in them.

During bunk searches, which the inmates call house raids, the COs move quickly. If they think you have contraband, they can toss your cell or your bunk without warning. They come in hot, overweight and out-of-breath, like second-hand SWAT, unannounced and sweaty, bearing hints of Old Spice amalgamated with McDonald's coffee breath.

The guards look forward to trashing the bunks. They shovel through your valuables like raccoons in a junkyard. It's inhumane, and it's meant to be. It's a formality to remind you that you are not in control. Some of the guards delight in the opportunity to confiscate personal items that have no extrinsic value, like drawings or magazine clippings. They do this just to remind you who wears the pants. They do this because they can. Often COs are men who have never been in positions of power themselves. I can tell they've had hard lives. I can tell they don't take care of themselves, mentally or physically. I get the impression many of them were bullied their whole lives, and now they finally get to be the bully (and get paid for it).

House raids are often calculated. The guards do it more to inmates they don't like. It's their way of flexing, reminding us they wear the badges and we wear the numbers. They move fast because it can put them, as well as other inmates, in a vulnerable position. When a CO is searching someone's bunk, their back is turned to everything else, and the inmates know that.

Getting your bunk tossed is a dirty, dehumanizing thing. It's not much of a bunk to begin with, but it's the only space you have. The blankets are wool, moth-eaten, and ragged. The pillows are hard and feel like armchair decor one might find in the dollar bin at Goodwill. Sheets are stained with the body odor of men twenty years before us and have brown spots from where they were tied to the rusted, metal bunks. Nevertheless, it's all we got…but the COs don't care. They toss everything you have on the ground, making sure to step on your valuables in the process. It's a good reminder that nothing is permanent. It's a good reminder that you are not your possessions.

In prison, everything is temporal. It's the opposite of stillness. It's the opposite of meditation. It takes you right out of your body and into the heat of anger and anxiety. When my bunk gets searched, I try to breathe through the anger. I try to breathe through the invasiveness. Nothing is private in prison. Nothing is yours.

When it happens, I feel that ball of energy in my lower back begin to throb, but I put my headphones on, look down at my radio, and stare at all the little pieces on the circuit board. I breathe through the invasiveness. I breathe through the moment. I look into my radio; I can see right through its plastics parts. Sometimes, I think my radio helps me channel the Divine energy that see through me too.

I close my eyes and listen to the sound. The static is not sharp or eerie, but calming. The sound feels thick and smooth like butter. I imagine that I'm standing in the sound, waist-deep, feeling it undulate around me. The sound is an ocean, and I am a wave.

In moments, I am back in that same cafeteria. I am staring at my thirteen-year-old self. He's looking at me and up at those same lights, drifting across the empty space above us. He is trying to process it. He is trying to process how I can see those lights too, because he thought he was the only one who could see them.

"Do you want to get out of here?" I ask.

I'm not sure why I ask him, but I feel compelled to. I feel the words slip out of my mouth like they aren't just my words but both our words, mine and my younger self.

"Where would we go?" he asks.

"Anywhere," I respond. "Anywhere safe."

"Anywhere?" he pauses. "Is this a dream?"

"I'm not sure. It doesn't feel like a dream, does it? It feels more real, but I don't really know."

"Okay," he says.

"Where do you want to go?" I ask.

He doesn't say anything, but I know where he wants to go, because it's where I want to go too.

I am not sure how it happens, but the sound and lights carry us. The static from my headphones begin to wrap around us, this younger part and this present part of me. Though I am still in my body on this bunk in this prison, we are transported somewhere else. We are transported to a river.

The Umpqua River meets the Pacific Ocean just outside of Reedsport, Oregon, passing under Highway 101, the coastal highway. It wends its way east below of Eugene, before it turns south toward the border of California, stopping shy of Grants Pass in Southern Oregon. I spent time on the Umpqua with my family at our close family friend's cabin.

After college, my friends and I used to have our annual guys' trip there along the river. In my twenties, the river became a sacred place. It was a place for kayaking, rafting, tubing, and swimming. For cooking, watching stars, and reading books in the dry summer air. It was a place for camping out and learning Tom Petty songs on our guitars. For eating good food and smoking baby blue American Spirits. The river was the spot where we felt safe enough to share secrets and talk honestly.

At night, we would carry our chairs down to the river, watch the stars, and listen to the music of the trickling water and chirping crickets. We'd drink beers and smoke pot, blaring music from bands like Wilco or the National through our Bluetooth speaker. Somehow, the weather was always perfect. The warm air juxtaposed by the coolness of the river meshed perfectly. It was a sacred, simple time.

As I got older, I realized the river was what made it sacred. The river was a part of us too. When I shared my secrets, it was the river I was talking to as much as my friends;

this river had been there for me through everything too. She was listening in ways my friends couldn't. She was listening in ways nobody could.

She never judged, only listened and flowed and spoke. Sometimes, early in the morning, I would wake up before my friends, pour a cup of coffee, and go down to the river to be alone. I'd sit on the seaweed-covered rocks, warmed by the morning sun, and talk to the river while sipping my coffee. Eventually, I'd roll up my pants and wade knee-deep in the water, feeling the current against my legs. I'd feel every rock underneath me and every ripple of water. The river would become my prayer; it would become a part of me. Soon, there would be no difference between me and the river. Planted as a seed on its banks, I would become a small tree, just observing the light refracted from the water. I'd dance and play and become a kid again.

The river remains sacred, as does the water, even now. She holds me in her palms and grounds me in ways no temple or church or city could. She holds an ancient wisdom, something that comes long before us and will remain long after us too.

In a small way, I think we all know we come from the Earth. We are born into her clay. The divine manifested into physical form from molecule to molecule, quark to quark. We come from the divine. We are all sacred life transformed by a loving Universe. The land pulls me in, the heat of the sun above and the heat of the earth below. Just like this river, my meditation shows me a glimpse of who I have been, who I always have been — the sticks and feathers and dried seaweed stuck in hot branches. The summer breeze, cool and low on the nape of my neck. The current of the river, the coolness of the water, its breath and its words. They are my brothers and sisters. The river has a very familiar sound to it. It's almost as if I can hear it when I close my eyes.

My younger self and I are standing at the bank of an island of rocks looking out at the Umpqua. There are green bushes and shrubs along the bank with old birds' nests sticking out of them, and the water is warm and colorful. The rocks are hot from the sun but smooth and soft beneath our feet. The river is gentle but also strong; it is alluring and spiritual. The water flows as it flows, not rigid or stern. It does not demand or require.

I look out at the water, and I can feel it looking back at me.

Neither of us say anything, but we don't have to. I am a witness. I am an observer.

I watch my thirteen-year-old self pick up a small, round rock and walk to the edge of the water. He curls his arms back and snaps his wrist forward to skip the rock across the river. It skips five or six times before diving beneath the surface.

"Nice one," I find myself saying to him.

He looks back at me with his big brown eyes, still curious, still unsure. He picks up another one and walks back to the water's edge.

"Who taught you to skip rocks?" I ask, already knowing the answer.

"My dad," my younger self replies. "He used to give us a quarter per skip."

I smile. It's the first non-sarcastic answer he's given me.

"So, who are you?" he asks.

I pause momentarily.

"Do you really want to know?" I respond eagerly.

"God, no!" he quips before skipping another rock.

Well, that didn't last long, I think to myself. I just keep getting dissed by younger me.

Eh…not much has changed.

"Knock, knock, inmate."

Suddenly I hear a rasp from somewhere above me. The sound of the water quickly fades, and I'm pulled up out of the depths of myself and the depths of the river. I open my eyes and see a guard at the foot of my bunk. His keys are jangling at his waist, and he's rattling the side of the metal bunk with his knuckles. I pull off my headphones.

"Get up. It's time to toss your bunk."

I get up to get out of his way.

"I need to check your radio," he says to me as I pass him. I slide my headphones off from around my neck and hand him my radio. He shakes it like a pack of Tic-Tacs before handing it back to me.

"No contraband in there, right?" he asks.

"None sir," I respond.

"Good. Now get out of here," he says to me as he slides on a pair of black disposable gloves.

I walk over to the tables in the day room, a common area the size of a small studio apartment. It's a poor excuse for a common area, like the lobby at a welfare office, with a few round tables, plastic chairs, and televisions mounted to the wall. There's no volume or sound on the TVs. That's what the radios are for. The TVs are linked with certain stations on the radio. You have to flip to the right station to hear the TV, but it's usually just old reruns of King of the Hill, Fox News, Cops (ironically), and MTV.

I flop down in one of the plastic chairs and put my headphones over my ears, but I don't turn on the radio. I have no desire to watch Cops or any other shows on Cable. I pretend to listen to my music, but instead, I eavesdrop on one of the conversations happening at the next table.

An inmate who goes by the name Smalls is sitting at a table with another inmate. He's chewing on an old toothpick and flipping through a deck of cards. Smalls, ironically, is at least six feet, six inches and weighs at least 250 pounds. He's one of the only other people of color in the dorm. He rides with the Blacks. From what I can tell, he seems to be well-liked by the other inmates in his car. I'm not sure how much time he's serving, but I get the feeling he's been down a while. He keeps to himself. He knows the routines. He knows when to keep his head down and when to blend in, which is hard thing to do if you're Black or Brown in a place like this.

I watch Smalls look over at my bunk and then back across at me. He gives me a nod. It's the best he can do. I don't ride in his car. All he can offer is a nod, but it tells me everything I need to know. It's an acknowledgement that says, you aren't Black, but we are the same — targeted in here and out there, too. He turns to the other inmate at the table.

"Looks like they got Li'l Mod," he says, referring to me (which I think is short for little Muhammad). "Mother fuckers better not toss my shit, or I might just go off. Locks and socks and shit."

Suddenly I hear my name from the CO. He's done with

my bunk, and he's waving me over. I walk back to my bunk. The guard has only a few things in his hands, which means they're being confiscated. They're nothing I can't live without, a few rubber bands, an old bookmark that doesn't have my ID on it, and a plastic tub.

"That's mine," I say to the CO, pointing at the tub.

"You're only allowed to have one," the CO responds.

"Sir, that's not what I was told," I respond as politely as I can.

"I don't care what you were told," he says.

I let it go. There's nothing I can do.

I go back and sit on my bunk. I lay against the metal bars and watch the CO walk off and out of sight with my plastic tub. After some time, I pull my headphones back over my ears and turn up the volume. The static vibrates within me like birds chirping in a wild jungle. The humming of the white noise creates a rhythm in me, much larger than my body. I feel like I am growing roots down into the earth below me, pushing through all the concrete and metal and plastic.

I begin to feel myself pushing through the earth all the way down, past dirt and soil, down into water. As I listen to the static of my headphones grows louder in my ears, I can feel myself push against the water and push against the mushy soil, almost as if I am pushing outward against something. But I'm going inward.

Soon the soil gives way and a flood of water comes rushing into the hollow space. I can feel my spine relax as I sit up straight against the metal bars of my bunk, but I am still deep below the sounds of water. I feel the water rise up above me, but I do not panic. It is welcoming and familiar. This water is family. I feel it swirling around the ball of energy in my lower back, like clouds around the sun.

I begin to swim out underneath this vast meditated sea. There are no creatures. No seaweed, kelp, anemones, or rocks — only water. I feel myself swimming toward the center of something wonderful, a beaming light within me. I stop to feel the water. It is the same temperature as my body. I stretch out my arms but no longer feel them, not because they are tired but because they feel now like they are made up of the water around me. It feels like the river.

All is peace.

Then, I hear a voice within.

It's okay.

"What's okay?" I respond.

It's okay to ask.

"To ask what?" I inquire.

To ask for help. No one will know. You can ask. I won't tell anyone I helped you.

The voice disappears, and it's just me in the water, floating peacefully in the nothingness.

Ask for help? No one will know? What does that mean? I wonder what it means, but I have no idea. The thought is frustrating.

Ask for help? I respond. No one is going to help me here. Who's asking for help? Who do I ask for help from? I find myself saying to the water.

Before there is an answer, I hear a loud echoing, only it's not coming from the water. It's coming from the dorm. I open my eyes and take off my headphones. Down beyond my bunk at the end of the dorm, I see a fight erupting. It's Smalls, and he's shouting at a CO.

I get off my bunk and stand near the bedpost to look down the dorm. I see an inmate standing between Smalls and the CO, restraining Smalls from swinging at the guard. I see Smalls, kicking and trying to fight his way back to the CO.

"Hell no, motherfucker," Smalls yells at the CO. "This ain't fucking right, bitch. You know! You know that you're targeting me. First little Mod, now me… the only two mother fuckers that ain't White. I see you, you fucking cracker."

I look at the CO, and he's calling for back up. He has a radio in one hand and what looks like a crumpled-up piece of paper in the other, but he's not scared. He's smirking. He looks happy with himself. This CO is known for being a blatant racist. He doesn't hide it. In fact, he flaunts it because he knows there's nothing we can really do about it. As long as he's careful, he can get away with it.

I hear Smalls yell again.

"Man, this ain't right. It's just a fucking photo, man. Come on, CO."

The CO unfolds the crumpled-up piece of paper with his black disposable gloves and reveals a photo.

"Who's this?" I hear the CO ask him with a hint of jealousy.

"That's my girl, man. Fuck. That's my photo. Can I have my photo?" Smalls shouts.

"Against protocol to have a photo that's not on the bulletin board provided. You had it taped to the back of your bunk, inmate. You know that's illegal, and I can write you up and confiscate your contraband."

"That's not contraband, man. That's my fucking wife.

That's a photo of my fucking wife, man."

The CO doesn't say anything. He just stares back at Smalls with a subtle smirk. A moment later, three COs come rushing toward Smalls with radios and handcuffs.

"What the fuck, man?" Smalls yells loudly.

"Place your hands behind your back," says one of the COs. "It's just a formality, Smalls. You didn't swing, but we gotta arrest you. You'll be out of the hole in no time, I'm sure."

"The fuck I will be," Smalls screams. "I didn't even fucking do anything, and you're putting me in the hole?"

The COs handcuff Smalls and walk him up the dorm toward the door. As he walks past my bunk, Smalls glances at me for a moment, and I hear him mumble something to himself before he shouts loudly, "Man, the lid on this jar is too fucking tight."

Then I watch silently as the COs march him out of the dorm, up the stairs, and out of sight toward the hole.

R.G. Shore

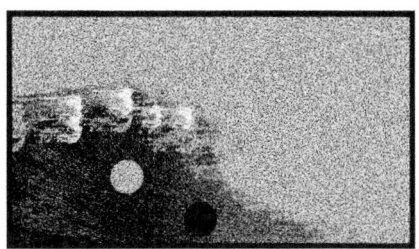

Meditation

My friends,

I'm not sure we can address the macro injustices until we can learn to sit with the micro ones. The two are not mutually exclusive nor are they any less important than each other. The injustices we feel on a global scale are the same injustices we hold within ourselves. The violence and pain we experience in the cities and in the prisons is the same violence and pain we experience in our own body. It flows in our blood, through our nervous system, and metastasizes across every city and capitol building. We hold onto these injustices because we don't know what else to do with them. The pain can feel too real. We learn to push it deep down inside of us and hide it. And then, we screw the lid tight on the jar. Meditation invites us inward to a place where we learn to loosen it, bit by bit.

Meditation teaches us to sit with the wound and injustice instead of continuing the pattern of avoidance or perpetuation of the injustice. When you learn how to sit with the younger parts of yourself, they will begin to open to you, but this can take time. In my experience, my younger self had no idea who I was. It was like looking through a veil at a stranger. At first, he didn't want anything to do with me, but the more time I spent with him, just listening and being there, the more he became curious. Eventually he was okay with me being in the same space as him. This did not happen overnight; it took months. So, be patient with yourself.

After a long time of meditating and being with my younger self, he finally felt safe enough to take me with him to a place he was comfortable being open and vulnerable in. I do believe this will happen for you, but you have to be willing to set aside any motivation for this to happen. In order for your younger parts to feel safe and vulnerable, you have to be vulnerable too.

All the parts of you, young and old, have experienced injustices. The further injustice is that no one has ever validated those parts of you. It is important to sit with your younger self and validate these parts so that they can feel seen and listened to. I cannot tell you what this exact process will look like for you because it will be a different for each human being based upon their own experiences, past wounds, and traumas.

There is a noticing first — an observance, a grieving, and an allowing that must take place. It is important that your younger parts don't feel like you're trying to fix them, and you shouldn't. The misconception is that you need fixing at all. There is no fixing necessary because you are already wholly who you need to be. When you come to realize this within your own body, that is the beginning of compassion. You are exactly who the Universe wants you to be; you are a part of it all.

My friends, be compassionate with yourselves and be willing to hold the "both/and" within you. You are not just your traumas, your fears, and your shames. You are not just a decaying body or skin woven tightly over memories you wish you didn't have. You are a vibrant light that never fades, a divine energy that began long before your smaller self. You are a star that eternally burns and outshines all shadow. This is the zenith of compassion: to be seen.

See yourself

In your meditation, find a quiet, safe space, a place you will not be interrupted.
After five to ten minutes of breathing, inhaling and exhaling, rising and falling, be still in your body.

How do you know when you are still?

In my experience, stillness arises when we begin to crave silence. It is a craving of rest, a craving of being allowed to just be. When you begin to feel the stillness arise in you, invite your younger self:

> I invite you here.
> All the parts of you.
> You are safe. You are welcome.
> It's okay to leave any time you'd like.
> I am here.

This invitation will look different for you than for another, so be willing to go with the flowing current inside yourself. Only you will know what your younger self needs to feel safe and welcomed. Over time, your younger self will in fact let you in, and it's important at that time to be gentle. When you feel ready, you can ask your younger self if they are willing to share their wounds with you. Maybe they will; maybe they won't, and that's okay. Remember, the wound you are asking them to share is your own. Perhaps, it is a wound that belongs not just to your younger self, not just to you, but to everyone. This is the micro, and this is the macro.

Chapter Eight

Fake Plastic Cheese

I'm sitting on my bunk with the idiot box on, flipping through channels aimlessly. I can feel myself staring off into nothing. The commercials on cable are all the same: overproduced music and cheap makeup, shows made up of people talking loud and unapologetically. I watch an advertisement for Facebook, AT&T, Tesla, and then a few local car commercials, followed by one for Amazon. The digital world is swirling all around, and we don't have any access to it. There are some men in here who don't know what smart phones are. We still have telephone booths with hook switches and dial tones in here — we call them stress boxes because that's all they are. It's already a tough enough battle getting out, but with the exponential growth of AI and technology, it'll make it near impossible for formally incarcerated people to navigate the world they'll be released to.

I look outside the window and see the fir trees in the distance just outside the fence. I watch them sway in the salted wind, careless and unadulterated by cable TV and social media. For a brief moment, I picture the trees staring in at me curiously, like cats looking in at a fishbowl.

I chuckle out loud thinking about the absurdity of the juxtaposition. The earth has a raw kind of love to it. She doesn't care about social media or whether or not our packages arrive with same-day delivery. She puts life into perspective. I look out at the trees and the old growth. I see mint green moss rising up alongside the bark like they're old friends. Some of these trees stand one hundred feet tall. I wonder how long they've been there. I wonder about all the things they've seen. I wonder about all the storms, rain, and sun they've experienced. I wonder how many people they've witnessed come through these walls. I watch some of the needles fall with the wind. They seem to be talking to each other in their wooded silence.

I am not a druid: I don't believe that trees are God, but there is certainly something divine about them. The Universe passes through them as it passes through me. You have to be able to see it everywhere, before you can see it anywhere.

Christians call it Christ, a divine energy that predates all energy. I call it the Universe. Some people call it spirit. I call it Qi or Prana. It's a life force beneath all things, in all things, moving all things, allowing all things, and loving all things. For some reason, I see it better in the earth than I do in people. I see it better in animals too. There's something animals understand that we just don't. We have to learn it through suffering, but animals instinctually know it, I think. The earth allows suffering and loss, and expresses it through her seasons. The Universe embraces the dying of stars, the equinoxes, and the phases of the moon. But the earth feels so distant from me now, like I'm on some plastic metal planet looking at it from afar. The touch of a tree feels like a lifetime ago.

I turn back to my TV and the four o'clock news is on. Nothing good, of course. One of the anchors announces there's a meteor shower around 10 p.m. Pacific Standard Time. I hear a few of the inmates in the dorm react. We are killers, thieves, domestic abusers, manipulators, liars, and racists — but we are also human, and we love our meteor showers.

There's a strict rule about not going outside past 9 p.m. We have to be quiet and in our bunks. I watch some of the inmates walk past me and approach the guard on duty. One of the inmates has a large "J316" tattoo (which I can only assume is in reference to the gospel passage John 3:16) above his eyebrow that hovers just above two tatted teardrops. I can hear them talking to the guard about the meteor shower, and one of them asks if they can just step outside the door tonight and watch it. The guard doesn't flinch but continues to read his magazine.

"If I can't watch it, you can't watch it," I hear him say without looking up.

The men look defeated and pissed off. I watch them walk past me and kick my bunk. The one with the tattoo says, "fucking faggot." I sigh and almost laugh at the absurdity. I have no idea how the guard not letting them watch the meteor shower makes me a homosexual (I know they're just venting their frustrations); in a place like this, two plus two equals chicken nuggets.

I've gotten better at not reacting, but I'm also human. And it's hard not to. I can still feel my body tense up and my neck get hot when I'm assaulted — maybe that's why I love the earth and animals the way I do. They've never intentionally hurt me or let me down.

The love my childhood dog had for me feels a lot more unconditional than any love I ever experienced inside a religion. I think about my dog's black curly hair, knotted and caked with dirt and grime from the farm. Whenever she saw me, she'd wag her tail with vigor, stick out her tongue, and fall into me like I was the safest thing in the world.

I remember going to a church group in college, and the pastor talking about salvation in a hackneyed kind of way. I remember his diatribe about souls and how humans were the only one of God's creation to have souls, (the kind of rhetoric one might hear alongside phrases like, "God the Father is a man," or "Men should have power over women.")

Then, in typical preachy fashion, he summarized the bullet points for what I imagined was his own private Calvinist indoctrination program:

"If you don't accept Jesus into your heart, then you won't go to Heaven." It was very fear-based and shaming, but he said it with a PNW smile and included the words, "God loves everyone…. *Love the sinner, hate the sin.*"

The words felt threatening and imperializing. I could tell they were coming from a place of power, control, and exclusivity. The words. "if you don't do this, then…" should never be spoken in congruency with love.

I remember raising my hand in front of all the other college students and asking him why he believed animals wouldn't be in Heaven. His response was as predictable as his long, bleach-blonde hair, "Because it's not in the bible."

The answer was ridiculous. Here was a man who had completely separated being Christ-liked from incarnation. Here was a man who got paid to preach the "Good News," but none of it was good. He couldn't see it in anything, so he certainly couldn't see it in everything. It felt plastic and cheap. I looked around the room to see if anyone else was seeing all the holes, but all I saw were smiling, White faces listening intently. I felt so different in that moment. I felt so isolated.

I think that's when I knew I couldn't go back. I think that's when I knew the whole thing was a house of straw. There was something happening in my Brown body back then in a way that I couldn't put into words. Somehow my body instinctually knew there was a deeper wisdom holding me — a wisdom that included so much more than what was being offered. When I think about animals and the earth, I can't help but see Christ in them in a much more profound way. The Christ in my dog feels like a much easier Christ to grasp than the one being marketed by a blonde, sheltered conservative in skinny jeans who smelled of coffee and capitalism. Little by little, my college years began to unveil the real apocryphal nature of American Evangelicalism. I began to see that it was just another product like something you could buy or squeeze through a tube.

I turn back to my TV and switch it off. I wasn't really watching it anyway. I try not to have it on for the most part. TV jumbles your brain. It makes you feel like a drunk monkey on acid. In the Buddhist tradition, they call it monkey mind because your thoughts are like monkeys jumping from branch to branch. The TV colors, bright lights, and frames-per-second make me dizzy. I try to sit in silence, but it's never silent here. It's never quiet. For a moment I try to remember what silence feels like, and I almost work myself into a panic.

People begin to move around me quickly. It's dinner time, which means the men are hungry. Prison food is always shitty, but when it's especially shitty, many of the cars make dinner in the dorm. The smells of greasy microwaved food blended together makes me nauseous. After a while though, it all smells the same no matter what you put into it.

Many of the men spread, which is a term for mixing food together. It's often a combination of soups (ramen), cheese paste, instant refried beans, and tubed meat.

Sometimes, they make fried rice. People get creative with what they have. The men who have been down decades have gotten innovative with the little resources.

I watch one of the cars begin to spread at a table nearby. I watch as he takes large tortillas held in magazine rolls and pile spoonfuls of god-knows-what onto them. Burritos are wrapped up in old newspapers or magazines to give them form. Then they're put under pillows to allow them all to melt together.

It's true, you have to get creative. I once made poor man's orange chicken by melting lemon heads in hot water, adding some honey packets and candy orange slices (the orange slices that are sticky, get caught in your teeth, and cause death breath). Then I mixed in spices with the help of some old ramen packets, crushed up Flamin' Hot Cheetos, and let it set overnight. It wasn't very good; I got sick from the chicken.

Everything tastes like plastic, including the cheese. You can buy packets of melted cheese that have the consistency of toothpaste. They look like a combination of melted plastic and dog shit. The men call it "squeeze cheese." It's the kind of cheese that goes straight through you.

There are three important lessons I've learned about spreading. First, don't trust the meat. Second, don't trust the cheese. And third, don't trust other people, which is why I spread alone. Like everything else, cars stick to their own when cooking meals. The Pisas make meal with the Pisas, the Whites with the Whites, and so on. I watch it all take place, divided up by race. The smell of plastic cheese and instant carbs begins to make me feel sick. The smell seeps into my skin like greasy food from the county fair. This place feels like a carnival without the rides or games.

I close my eyes and put my headphones over my ears, but the smell of plastic cheese comes wafting into my bunk area. I listen to the static, and I turn the volume up on my radio. I take a few deep breaths. I inhale slowly and breathe through my nostrils. I pause and let the static turn to water.

I'm on a beach that looks like the Oregon Coast. The ocean is lined with trees and rocks. The air is salty, the wind heavy, but it's not raining. I walk out a few steps into the water. Slowly the waves start to fold in on me. I look down, and the waves begin to turn orange... the color of cheese.

Dammit.

I open my eyes to the smell of burnt nachos and plastic rubber. I slide my headphones off and pull my sweatshirt over my nose to try and conceal the smell. It doesn't work. I start to get angry. I feel energy pulling at me from inside. I feel myself pulled up into my head and out of the center that usually holds me.

Meditation isn't easy. Sometimes I feel like I'm dropping a seed in an outhouse just hoping for a fruit tree to grow. As I breathe in, I remember the secret lies within the body. Trust the process. I have to get out of my head and back into my body. I look down and focus on my hands. I look at my skin. The dry skin looks like scales. I try to look closer, breathing deeper with every inhale and exhale. The skin patterns look like tectonic plates sliding up against each other. I look at my fingers and then my fingernails. I watch my fingers slowly turn orange, like Cheetos...

I hate the smell.

In meditation, everything is used. Meditation isn't the

escape from reality but the allowing of it. Meditation is allowing reality to be what it is — I know this — but to embody it is a completely different task. The cheese just is. The noxious smell just is. I remember hearing a story about a man who travelled halfway across the world to be at a retreat with a well-known sadhu, or yogi, from India. When he got there, the man was head over heels to learn that he was going to be able to get a few minutes alone with the sadhu.

When the man approached the yogi, he asked him just one question. "How do I find —" but before he could finish his question, he heard the loud sound of a chainsaw in the distance from a neighboring farm. Some local workers were cutting large culms of bamboo. The man waited patiently for the chain sawing to stop.

When they finally stopped buzzing, the man continued to ask his question.

"Holy Sadhu, I was just wondering, how do I find peace? I meditate for two hours daily, but still, nothing happens —".

As he finished the question, the chainsaws began to buzz again. The man grew angry.

"For God's sake," he thought.

He had travelled halfway across the world for a few minutes with one of the holiest men in the entire world, and he wasn't about to let a bunch of chainsaws ruin it. He got up quickly, stepped outside, and yelled at the top of his lungs, "Can't you see we're trying to have a retreat here?"

Afterwards, he went back and sat down with the sadhu to finish his thought.

"I am so sorry, Sadhu. I just can't stand the noise."

The sadhu looked at him and smiled brightly. He didn't speak, but only smiled. After a few moments, the man, again, began to grow impatient as he waited for an answer. Finally, the sadhu broke his silence.

"Live like the bamboo," replied the yogi.

"I don't understand.," replied the man.

"Don't push against the chainsaws."

I try not to push against the chainsaws, but mine are either racist and have swastika tattoos or they're orange and smell like plastic.

There is always so much busyness, beeping, buzzing, man-made sounds here. The intercom is always blaring. The microwave is always being slammed shut. People are always yelling at football games on their TVs. Chairs squeak obnoxiously as they continuously scrape across the floor.

I decide to take a much deeper breath and hold it. Just observe it, I tell myself. I look around at everyone moving about, trying to make sense of it all. There is no stillness here — none.

As I observe, I begin to see and notice patterns. I watch one inmate continue to walk in circles around his bunk. He picks up a book, flips it open, stands at the end of his bunk, and pretends to read. He's not really reading; I notice him watching one of the tables in the day room where the Natives sit. Then I watch him close his book, go back to the end of the dorm, and say something to some other inmates in his car.

I watch him do this two or three times. Finally, on the third time, he puts down his book and heads for the table. As he walks past the table, he snags two meat sticks that belong to the other car and hides them in his sleeves. Then I watch him walk away without anyone noticing. This place really is a den of thieves.

A few minutes later, I see the Natives at the table begin to freak out. I watch as one inmate stands up, looks around the table, underneath it, and around the chairs. I start to see the panic in him as he realizes he's lost his food. He begins to curse loudly. One of the other Natives approaches him. I can't hear exactly what he's saying, but I know the gist of it.

I'd help him out if I could, but that's looked down upon. Even if it's out of kindness, you don't go and give something freely to someone else because it can be taken as a threat. After all, this place is a *now you owe me* kind of place. Plus, you don't mess around with people in other cars, which makes it difficult for me because I'm not in a car. I usually make the joke that I'd rather bike anyway — it's more eco-friendly. I feel bad for the guy, but then I realize that I can't help him out anyway because of my first and second rules of spreading.

After a few moments, I see one of the Natives go back toward his bunk, grab something, and bring it back to the table — two more meat sticks. He hands it to the Native and smiles.

"I got you," he says.

This I hear clearly. Sitting on my bunk, watching it all take place, I realize this is also meditation. It is not separate from it. It's not separate from what I experience with my headphones on. Divinity is not separate from everything else. We are divine, and we are human too. We are the stealing of meat sticks and the giving of meat sticks. The reality is polarizing because it's both/and. In all this racism and deception and plastic, there is still a quality that makes us human — not much, but it's there. I put my headphones on and turn up the static. I pull my wool beanie over my eyes, lay down, and fall asleep.

I wake up to the sound of music. The dial on my radio must have brushed up against something. The FM signals are still static, but I can hear a faint song coming through my headphones. I sit up and pull my beanie back up over my eyes. It's dark out; I've missed dinner. People are sleeping around me. I begin to fidget with the dial on my radio. I move it up and down with my thumb until I hear the song come in clearer.

I recognize the music. I recognize the lyrics. It's an acoustic version of Radiohead's Fake Plastic Trees. The song is too perfect. The Universe couldn't have planned it any better. I listen to the lyrics and allow the vibrations of the song to sink deeply into my bones:

Her green plastic watering can
For her fake Chinese rubber plant
In the fake plastic earth

That she bought from a rubber man
In a town full of rubber plans
To get rid of itself

It wears her out
It wears her out
It wears her out
It wears her out

Tears begin to form in my eyes. I feel the numbness burning off. I feel the rubber in me burning off. Suddenly, there's a rasp at my bunk. I look up, and it's the night guard.

"Hey," he says. "The Lieutenant wants to see you."

The chain of command in prison is based on the military ranking system (no wonder why the whole thing is so fucked up): Correctional Officers, Sergeant, Lieutenant, Captain. I've never met or even seen the Captain. It's a big deal if the Lieutenant wants to see you. It usually means you're in trouble, especially this late at night. Sometimes it means you're getting new charges or you're being shipped off to another prison. It's not protocol, but it does happen.

I slide my radio off and tuck it under my pillow. I make my bed (we're always required to before we leave). I put on jeans and a jacket and my shoes. I head outside of the dorm and up the stairs toward the first gate. There are several gates in prison. The first gate gets us out of the yard, up the stairs, and into the common grounds of the prison. This is how we get to places like chow or medical, or to administration.

I get to the gate and push the intercom. Immediately, I hear a voice.

"What?"

"I think the Lieutenant wants to see me."

"Number?" I give him my SID number, which is a number assigned to all inmates. Again, the whole thing is incredible dehumanizing. They might as well pierce tags behind our ears and call us cattle.

The gate buzzes open, and I head up a larger set of stairs toward the admin building. There's a building with a glass panel in the front (bullet proof I imagine) and an officer sitting behind the panel at a microphone. He leans forward and speaks through the glass.

"Around the corner. First door on the left. Knock. Then when the Lieutenant says you can, enter."

I feel like I'm at a fraternity house. The whole thing is archaic and strange — a speakeasy for inmates. I head around the corner and knock on the first door on the left. After a few moments,

I hear the Lieutenant from inside.

"Come in," he yells from behind the door.

I open the door and walk into the building.

"Inmate approaching," I hear another officer yell.

I walk around the corner and into a kitchen area, which must be the staff lounge. The room is much warmer than any other room in the prison. It almost feels human. There are donuts, muffins, and a family size carton of Starbucks on the table. I glance around the room and see a Keurig Coffee Maker, hot kettle, snacks, and popcorn. On the wall, I see a mounted board of at least thirty radios.

"In here," the Lieutenant says from a back office.

I walk back into his office, a larger space, like a corner office meant for a CEO. The Lieutenant is sitting at his desk. He wears a different uniform than other COs and sergeants with distinguished stripes on his shoulders. He looks sturdy, clean shaven, and well kept.

"Have a seat," he says to me. I sit. "So, I hear you're smart."

"Sir?" I respond, a little confused. I glance at the clock behind his computer: 9:55 p.m. I'm not sure why the Lieutenant has called me up to his office at ten o'clock at night just to ask if I'm smart, but I'm relieved I'm not in trouble.

"You're smart, yes?" he asks.

"Yes," I respond.

"Yes, *Sir*," he corrects me.

"Sorry, Sir. Yes, Sir," I respond.

"I hear you have a master's degree."

I nod my head yes.

"And you're here for another year or so?" he continues.

I nod again.

"Well, we are in need of a Law Clerk. They're called Law Librarians. Essentially, they help the inmates with all their legal needs. It's five days a week, but you get a computer. And it's quiet. Do you know anything about law?"

I shake my head no.

"Well, you'll train and study for a month or two and learn all the laws. Then you'll help the inmates with all their legal problems. They even have paralegal programs available out there for inmates, but you'd have to pay for those yourself. You interested?"

I nod. "Yes, Sir. I'm very interested. Thank you."

"Great," he replies. "You'll start Monday. Now, go back to the dorm. Close the door on your way out."

I walk out of the admin building, relieved and grateful. I'm not sure what I was expecting, but it wasn't that. I'm not sure what to make of it. It's way out of the blue, but it's something different. And it gets me out of the dorm.

I take a moment and breathe in the night air. The air is crisp and cold and feels good against my face. It's quiet. I take in as much as I can, savoring the solitude. The night feels open and alive. I can hear the sound of crickets chirping in the distance. For a moment, it almost doesn't feel like I'm in prison.

I look up into the sky and see the stars. They're bright and piercing. The air is open, and I can see the dark ocean far in the distance. The earth is still, but it's holding me here. Suddenly, I see a flash above me. I watch as a ton of stars begin to shoot across the sky. Then I remember about the meteor shower; I had completely forgotten.

No one is around me. I take my time heading back to the dorm, but I don't take my eyes off the sky. I watch the meteors fall across the night, and I smile. All is quiet.

Then I hear a subtle voice within me.

It will all work out. I got you.

R.G. Shore

PART II

Chapter Nine

The Doe

It's not dark at night here. In prison, dark means danger. The prison doesn't want people getting shanked in their sleep. At 9 p.m., red lights go on instead, which means, it's time to shut the fuck up (as the guards often say). The red glows in the hollow of the dorm, illuminating the room like the inside of a stop light. It's bright and makes it hard to sleep. I pull my beanie over my eyes and hope that nobody messes with my stuff… or my body.

I sleep on Front Street, which is right next to the day room, and the bathroom lights shine right into my face. Front Street is what they call the first row of bunks in front of the CO's desk. They put people who are in trouble on Front Street to teach them a lesson, but they also put people who are at risk for getting jumped as well. Being on Front Street means I'm safe, but it also exposes me to everything the night COs do, like flipping through ESPN apps or similar on their phones. At night, their phone screens light up against their faces and illuminate the whole dorm. If they're wearing glasses, I can see exactly what they're doing — often it's TikTok. The night COs also watch the TV in the day room, usually with the volume up louder than it needs to be. I've never seen someone so interested in late night infomercials for miracle mops.

On occasion, you get a CO who treats you like a real person. Guards are people too; they bring their own insecurities and traumas with them into the prison, whether they're aware of them or not. You can tell when a CO is lonely at home or insecure about their weight or about their social life. I remember hearing one of the guards tell another inmate, "The only difference between you and me is that I haven't gotten caught yet." (I think he was bragging about his frequenting meth use.)

Night is a good time to meditate, but even at night, it's never quiet or still. The snores echo through the dorm like an orchestra. I try to ignore them as I flop around my bed like a fish out of water. I allow my mind the pleasure of wandering for a while, but eventually I know I'll give in, sit up, and meditate instead.

I reach for my radio and begin by sitting up straight. I unwind my headphone chords from around my radio and plug them in. I take a few deep breaths. I breathe in deeper into my lower belly, and I can feel the pain pulsing somewhere in the depths. My pain is a kite, my breath its wind. I can feel it swaying about in different parts of my body. I try to notice it without judging it. I try to allow it without pushing it. The pain in my body warns me when I'm getting too close to a part of me that doesn't want to be discovered. My trauma creeps up in my body like a burglar in the kitchen.

Sitting up straight is important in meditation. Having a straight spine allows the energy in the body to move more freely up and down the spine, but I have bad posture. My lower back is always in pain; I can tell I'm holding something there, down in my low back. I can tell something is going on in that part of my body, and it needs to be released.

My breath begins to settle. My body begins to loosen. I invite the Universe in. Something is different this time. Usually, the meditation comes like an ocean within me, but this time I feel separate from it, like I am floating on its surface not fully immersed. I try slowing my breath, feeling its stillness. I aim for the kind of stillness one feels when they're out in a gentle snow, and all is calm, cold, and awake.

After a while of steady breathing, I begin to feel the air around me grow colder. The cold slowly morphs into a winter scene. The radio volume is low, and the snow comes in soft. The white snow covers a vast ocean before me. I can see a blanketed sea of ice, but I am not cold. The ocean is at a close distance. I am just a bystander peering into a window within me. The snow begins to fall thicker onto the frozen ocean. I am standing on an icy beach, the sand frozen and crunchy beneath my feet. The waves are barely moving, covered in ice. I look out at the frozen sea and can see through it like translucent glass. I step out onto the solid ocean, an aquarium beneath my feet. I watch the waves underneath me. Somehow the ocean still roars (a sign of the static blasting into my ears).

I turn and look in all directions. The beach is white. The ocean is white. The glass I am standing on, though translucent, is also white. I see the waves beneath the glass moving back and forth underneath me. The optical illusion dizzies me. It is moving, but I am not. I quiet myself out of the dizzying panic and look out before me. The ice brings a calmness, the cold brings me right into my body. I become more aware of the muscles within me as they begin to restrict due to the cold. I let out a strong exhale and see a bursting cloud of breath exit my mouth. All is calm. Time seems to stand still here.

I look up into the sky. Clouds overhead are gray, but I can see a pure light shining through them. The sky is raw and expansive. It opens before me like a desert sky. I feel closer to it.

The austerity of the ice beneath me and the spaciousness of the sky above me begin to amalgamate and become one. I cannot make out where sky begins and the sea ends. The cold brings a stillness that I haven't experienced in a while.

Suddenly I see something move out of the corner of my eye. I look over and in the cool distance, I see a deer walking out over the frozen ocean. Her fur is thick and matted in a brown-grayish hue, but at a distance it almost looks green. She stands elegantly against the white of the snow. I watch as she turns and looks at me.

On the top of her head, just between her eyes, I see a white patch of fur. In the middle of the white patch, I can see the shape of a U with a line across the top. Behind the U are two triangles, one pointing upward and the other downward, together making the shape of a star. There is a circle around the star shape lined with many petals. I've seen the symbol before. I recognize it, but I can't remember what it is:

The doe watches me calmly, and I watch her back. She stands gentle and still. I watch as she begins to walk slowly toward me, inching her way forward. As she comes closer, the pattern on her head becomes clearer.

I stand just feet away from her now. She brings a stillness I have never experienced before. She patiently watches me, and I patiently watch her back. I begin to observe everything. When she breathes nothing comes out — not even the air is disturbed by her presence. She is so peaceful. I stand across from her for some time, maybe an hour, but I'm not sure how long.

After some time in silence, the doe takes a few steps backwards. I look down and see a hole in the ice where she once was standing. The hole is large and cut in a perfect circle. I walk up to the hole and peer down through the ice. I can see the swirling white ocean underneath, its waves undulating back and forth beneath the glass.

Suddenly out of nowhere, the doe leaps down through the open hole and disappears into the ocean. As she hits the waves, she does not make a splash or a sound. Without thought, I make the choice to follow. I take a huge inhale and plunge headfirst through the hole in the ice, into the ocean waves beneath me.

I hit the waves with a splash and feel myself plunge below. The water is ice cold and sharp, and it stabs at me like ten thousand knives. I gasp and let out a huge breath of air. It's too cold. I can't think about anything but the sharpness of the water. I frantically look around and try to spot the doe underneath the water. My arms sway back and forth in a frozen panic. After several gasps, I spot her. She is several meters in front of me, swimmingly gently through the water. She doesn't look cold or disturbed by the numbing waves. Suddenly I hear a voice. The voice is soft and gentle. I think it's her:

Anahata — the only way to heal is through.

I don't know what it means, but I can't stay. I can't stay

and listen. I'm too cold. The pain is too sharp. I look at the doe and then back up at the hole in the ice above me. Somehow, I can sense she knows that I've already made the decision. She looks at me with her gentle eyes. She does not judge me. In fact, there is a small part of me that think she understands. I watch her for a moment before she turns and swims away. I immediately turn around the other way and swim for the hole in the ice above me. In a few painful arm strokes, I am back at the surface of the water looking up through the hole. Out of breath and frozen, I muster all the strength I have and pull myself up out of the ocean and back onto the wintery glass.

There's no hesitation; I pull my headphones off my ears and gasp. My meditation is over. I'm back on my bunk. I unplug my headphones from the radio and set them off to the side on my small bookshelf.

What the hell was that?

I sit cross-legged on my bunk and try to figure out what the meditation was about. It felt so real. I felt so deep in my body, but I'm not sure what it meant. I take a deep breath and try to compose myself. I pull my beanie up from over my eyes just in time to see the night CO approaching. Thankfully, it's a guard who is a little bit nicer.

"Hey what are you doing up?" the CO asks, waving his flashlight in my face.

"I was just meditating, Sir," I answer.

"Well, uh, you should be sleeping, not meditating."

"I couldn't sleep. It's too loud."

"Too loud?"

I point my finger around the dorm to all the snoring inmates.

"The chain saws," I respond.

The guard gives me a stiff smile.

"Yeah, can't help you there…"

"So, keeping up on the latest viral trends?" I ask jokingly, trying to lighten the mood.

"What?" the guard asks me.

"TikTok," I reply pointing to the phone in his hand. His face turns red. I can't tell if it's anger, embarrassment, or just the glow from the red lights in the dorm.

"I'm not on TikTok," the guard says defensively.

I watch him slide his phone back in his pocket. As he does so, I can clearly see the black and white TikTok app logo on the front of the screen. I knew it!

The guard continues to hover by my bunk awkwardly for a few moments.

"So, uh, meditation…that's a Buddhist thing?" he asks, trying to change the subject. "You a Buddha or something?"

He pronounces the word "Buddha" like "Buh-duh" (butter). My mind quickly draws an image of a stick of butter with legs in an orange robe, meditating and saying the word "Om" through its open-buttery mouth. I can't help but crack a smile.

"Sorry, Sir," I say. "Did you ask if I am a Buddhist?"

"Well, I thought you were Muslim, but when you said meditation, I figured maybe you're a Buddhist," the guard replies, still pronouncing the word like butter (buh-duh). "No offense or anything."

I'm not sure how to take his words. I know he means well. I know he's trying, like, actually trying, but the implications are inherently racist. I think for a moment whether it's a good time to address it. (It's never a good time for an inmate to address anything to a guard, so I choose not to.)

"No reason to think I'd be offended," I respond with a white lie. "No. I'm not Muslim. And I don't necessarily consider myself Buddhist either."

"Well, I got a Buddhist (buh-dist) joke for you," the guard says, completely ignoring my response and still managing to mispronounce the word.

"Okay," I reply with a cringe.

The guard delivers the joke with a chuckle, "So, a Buddhist walks into a Pizza Hut, and the pizza guy says, what you do want? And the Buddhist says, 'Make me one with everything.'"

I laugh painfully through my teeth.

"That's a good one," I pause. "Okay, I got one for you too, Sir," I respond trying to relate to him. "What did the Buddhist say when his landlord tried to kick him out of his apartment?"

"I dunno, what?" the guard asks.

"Namaste," I respond, laughing to myself. The guard doesn't react. Instead, he just stares at me blankly.

"I don't get it," he finally answers.

"Namaste… like… Nah, I'm gonna… Nevermind," I stop mid-sentence, giving up on my joke.

'Hmm… well, anyway… best be getting to bed," the guard replies.

"Do you mind if I stay up? I'm not really bothering anyone by meditating."

"You're not going to be loud, right? Like doing any of them Buddhist chants?" he folds his thumb and first finger into a circle, raises them up in a meditative position, and begins to mimic the sound "Om" with his mouth. This is another time I have to actively choose to just stay quiet. I shake my head no silently.

"Okay, fine. You can meditate. Just do it quietly."

As the guard walks off, I hear him say to himself… "Not a Muslim huh? Who would have thought."

It's now midnight, but still, it's not quiet. The inmate's snores echo loudly through the dorm, but they're not in sync. There's no pause or intermission between snores. When one inmate's snore begins to run out of gas, another inmate's starts up. It's like a never-ending cycle of lawn mowers.

The red lights of the dorm feel brighter now. I blame the snoring. I pull my beanie back down over my eyes and plug my headphones into my radio again. I want to do this. I want to find the doe and figure out what the meditation is about.

I turn the frequency to a louder channel of white noise. I crank the volume as loud as I can and hold my hands over my ears. I tell myself to breathe with it.

Just breathe with the static. Don't be afraid.

My inhale is extra-long and extra loud. I can tell there is a bit of panic underneath my breath. What if I get trapped under the ice? What if I can't find her? I know this is just a fear. I know better than to listen to the sound of my own thoughts, but sometimes I can't help it. I remind myself that my thoughts are just fish in a large stream.

Let them swim on past, I tell myself.

I take another inhale in. I try to let my breath lead me, instead of the other way around. I know it's not so much about controlling my breath as it is about letting my breath be what it is, and just going along for the ride. During meditation, I don't count sheep or inhales, I don't try to match my breaths with my heartbeat. There's no agenda other than just allowing myself to be present to what is.

My mind continues to wander. I think about the CO asking me if I'm a Buddha (buh-duh). I can't help but laugh thinking about a stick of butter dressed in orange Kasayas (Buddhist robes).

Don't think about butter, I tell myself. Don't think about butter.

My mind is awake, and I just can't shake it. Sometimes it doesn't have an off switch. I know I need to calm myself, to breathe deeply, and to follow my breath. I decide to practice an alternate breathing technique called Nadi Shodhana, a Pranayama exercise that helps balance the breath and helps to align the inner energy.

This alternate breathing technique has been around for thousands of years in the Yogi tradition. The Vedic tradition teaches that we have thousands of energy channels, called nadis, (perhaps something similar to meridians for acupuncture). There are three main nadis in our body that rise from our spine, starting at the base of the spine (the Muladhara, or sacral chakra): the Ida (the yin channel left of the spine), the Pingala (the yang channel right of the spine), and the Sushumna (the channel that follows the spine). The Ida and Pingala symbolize the feminine and masculine energies, or yin and yang energies. The Ida and Pingala rise from the sacral chakra, making their way to the nostrils, while Sushumna rises from the sacral chakra to the Sahasrara, or seventh chakra, at the crown of the head.

The alternate nostril breathing exercise is meant to

balance these energy channels. The nadis on both the right and left spiral up the body, crisscrossing in a double helix shaped fashion. This creates what's known as the dominant nostril concept, which makes it easier to breathe out of one side of the nose than the other. Throughout the day, the dominant nostril switches back and forth between Ida (yin) and Pingala (yang).

I sit up straight on my bunk, plug one side of my nose, and inhale for four seconds. I cover my right nostril with my thumb and forefinger and breathe into my left nostril. The sensation feels strange, like a vacuum or a straw. The air is thick as it rises into my nose. I count to four, and then I hold. I gently plug both my nostrils and try to feel what it's like to hold the breath in. It feels like I'm underwater. It's calmer, and I feel a sense of peace begin to float around my mind.

After sixteen seconds, I unplug the other side of my nose and breathe forcefully out. I repeat this breathing exercise for at least ten rounds. I'm trying to get back into my body.

I continue to hear the loud snores from the neighboring bunks. My head is so wrapped up in the anger and fear that I can feel being surrounded by all these men. I'm breathing to go back into my body, but it's hard. It's hard not to listen to the snores and the coughing. It's hard not to listen to the voice of panic within me. Like telling someone not to think about an elephant, all I can do is think about the sound of the snoring.

I breathe in again, focusing on the air coming into my nose. When I breathe in, I feel a warmth and a light. The light is red and blue. As the air travels up my nostrils, the warmth and light travel with it. When I hold the breath, the lights disappear. It feels like I've entered a cave. I'm on my last round breathing in, when suddenly, I see a different kind of light. It's not red, or blue. This light is brighter, like the brights on a car. I try to follow it as I count quietly to myself: one, two, three, four…hold for sixteen.

As I hold the sixteen counts, I can't help but follow the lights in. I can feel my body relaxing, and I can feel the weight of my shoulders begin to melt. I want to go with my breath; I want to allow it to take me where I'm supposed to go. I'm almost there, I can feel it. I imagine a large space opening up, hollowing my body like a bamboo shoot, giving a path for the oxygen to travel. I hold it there for as long as I can.

I sit here with my eyes closed. I try to imagine the icy ocean. I try to see the white glass and spot the doe — no luck. I can feel the energy trapped in my lower back. My attention goes there. I can see a light down deep within me. I squeeze it from my stomach and try to draw it upward from my belly into my third eye.

As I squeeze the light in me, the light outside of me begins to dissipate. The red lights begin to fade. The dorm is gone now. The snoring is gone too, and it's just me in this quiet space. I look around for the doe. I look for the snow-covered ocean, but I can't see it.

Suddenly, I see something, but it's not an ocean or a deer.

It's a house, hard to make out really. A small home maybe with some stairs, I don't know. There is a deck outside. It's a wrap-around deck. The house is brown, maybe? There are a lot of bushes and trees outside. It's beautiful. It's hard to make out any real detail, but then I see a figure: a younger woman, maybe in her thirties, dressed in black. She has long white-silver hair. I can't make out any other details. I'm not sure what her face looks like, exactly how old she is, or who she is. She's standing on a yoga mat outside on the deck and doing yoga poses in the sun. I've never seen her before, but the feeling she brings is familiar and warm. The image lasts maybe five seconds. Then, in a flash, it's gone, and I'm back again on my bunk. I switch off my radio, take my headphones off, and turn over to try to fall asleep amidst the storm of snores before me.

Meditation

My friends,

What awaits you beyond what you know?
Can you hold the pain that comes with mystery?

At this point in my journey, I was not sure what pain lay within me. This is the fear that comes with transformation: to leave the home we've always known and trust that we will still be led to where we need to go. The truth is, the ego is not all bad. The ego also acts as your protector. It protects you from the wounds that are too much to bear. Your ego wants to climb high, but it also wants to protect. The ego is a fragile giant; it wants to be loved and held in its own importance. In a world of death, the ego, above all else, strives to live.

Before prison, I thought I had to be somebody, and then when I wasn't, it was too devastating for me. I couldn't handle failure, but the divine within me knew the only way I could truly learn to let go was to fail again and again and again.

The true path to meditation means learning to let go of the one thing you thought you were supposed to do — and you have to let go of that completely. We hold onto our achievements, our accolades, and our titles because we think it gives us worth and value. We all want to belong. Most of us have grown up in a world that tells us our worth is dependent upon how much we can accomplish. This is ego capitalism: you must have something valuable to market and something tangible to contribute. In the end, you almost always end up marketing your very self.

We all want to find what we are looking for, but what if we don't like the answer that comes? We all want to be led until we realize we are being led to a place that we don't want to go. In my meditation, I was so captivated by the light of the doe within me, I wasn't cognizant of where she was taking me until it was too late; it was too much for my fragile ego to handle.

Confronting the ego means being very honest with yourself, which is hard to do. It means being vulnerable in a way that we are not accustomed to. This kind of reflection and honesty teaches us new ways of thinking and new ways of behaving. It teaches us to confront all the parts of ourselves and asks us to own our wounds and take responsibility for our actions, but also not to die there.

Letting go of who we never were — this is key. We have to be willing to sit with ourselves long enough to realize that maybe the thing we wanted wasn't what we needed. Or maybe, the thing we think we wanted wasn't what we wanted at all. Asking the hard questions exposes the underlying patterns, which opens our spirit to new possibilities and patterns for the future. Confronting the underlying patterns — how we see and how we respond — can be a very painful process. To go willingly into the shadow is not an easy task, but, my dear friends, this is exactly what we must do.

Hard Questions

Start by closing your eyes and asking yourself the following question:

If no one was around, who would you want to be?

Right away you might be tricking yourself into thinking you already know the answer, and it might be a good one!

Well, I want to do good things.

I want to help my community.

I want to be at peace.

I want to heal and serve others.

I want to be a teacher, a nurse, a gardener, an architect, or a marine biologist.

I want to write a book or act in a play.

I want to learn from animals. I want to grow plants and harvest the land.

I want to go to college. I want to go to law school. I want to change the system.

While these are all noble paths, notice, I did not ask what do you want to do? I asked, who do you want to be? The answer I don't know is a very real and very scary answer, but it's also a good place to start. So, be honest with yourself. Be patient with yourself and sit with the pauses, sit with the space between breaths.

Here are some questions you can ask yourself during meditation. These are challenging questions that can get you to a place of real honesty. You do not have to share your answers with anyone. It is most important to feel safe.

1. What if you never got to do what you thought you needed to do in this life? Would you be okay?

2. What if you never became who you wanted to be? Who would you be then?

3. What if you never could be great? What would your value look like?

4. What is the most important thing to you in the world? …Now, what if you lost it?

5. What if the person you loved most found out about your deepest wound? What if they still wanted to love you anyway? Would you let them?

6. What is one of your largest regrets? Can you invite it in, sit with it, and become friends with it?

7. What are you most ashamed of? Can you turn it into a gift?

The questions aren't about highlighting shame, fear, anxiety, or worry. The importance lies in the transformation that must take place in how you see yourself. Your value, your worth, your divinity is endless. You are not just all those things you thought you were. You were born before those things, and you will live after those things too.

These are identity questions meant to challenge you in a way to see beyond yourself. These are questions meant to challenge you to see value, not in the way that society sees value and not in the way religion sees value. Not the way politics, fame, nor even family sees value. The goal is let go of the need for approval from all these things and see that the highest form of yourself, the divine within you, the Universe, already wholly approves and loves you — regardless.

We live in a society that punishes us for our mistakes and makes us feel weak. We live in a society that teaches us to equate our hurt and our wounds with our very self. For most of my life, I equated myself with my shame. And when my shame became too much to bear, I became too much to bear. Prison taught me to see that grace comes in a form we often don't want, but she comes nonetheless. Grace comes to show us we are held in an energy much stronger than our shame and fear. She is the unexpected gift that is not dependent upon anything we do, say, or believe. She is our very breath, always falling, always rising.

Chapter Ten

Brown-Eyed Susan

The prison law library is a disheveled little room, the size of a storage unit. Inside, there are hundreds of old law books that line the shelves — books that haven't been touched in years, layered in dust. The spines are intimidating and thick, numbered from A-Z like encyclopedias. Scattered around the shelves are titles one might find in a Grisham novel: *Oregon Rules of Appellate Court, State Constitutional Law, Litigating Constitutional Law, Common Law 2nd Edition, Ninth Circuit Criminal Handbook, Legal Forms and Legal Research.*

The tone of the room is heavy and rigid, while at the same time rustic and unkempt. I can see cobwebs older than me in the corners of the top shelves. There are tons of old miscellaneous items that should have been tossed years ago: a deflated basketball, a stack of National Geographic magazines littered with bird poop and mice droppings, an old fan with a plastic bag over it shoved in the back corner next to a small window. The window doesn't peer outside, but only into an adjacent, larger room. There is no natural lighting in here. This place is an attic on the ground floor.

The computers must be from the '90s. They're blocky and white and have a startup button on the front of the monitor. Like everywhere else in prison, there's no connection to the internet. All legal research is done via books: publications, opinions, Oregon Administrative Rules (OARS), and Oregon Revised Statutes (ORS).

The prison also has access to an online system of legal

data through a program called LexisNexis, a legal database lawyers use to research laws, opinions, administrative rules, civil procedures, local rules, etc. The program feels outdated and clunky, like a digital platform you might find in a public library that still uses AOL.

I've been studying for several months now. The world of law is rigid and straight. There isn't room for color or nuance. It's a world of legal jargon from a dead language nobody uses. Often referred to as legalese, the language of law is blanketed with Latin terms in a way that keeps people from understanding their own rights. The pages are slathered with terms like "heretofor," "therein," "nunc pro tunc," and one of my favorites, "nemo dat quod non habet," — "no one can give what he has not." It's a very spiritual idea in theory but, unfortunately, primarily used in bankruptcy law. The more I study law, the more I begin to see why so many people incarcerated feel so trapped within the system.

Laws enacted through legislature in the State of Oregon are called Oregon Revised Statutes, or ORS. They are divided into volumes that are then subdivided into titles based upon the type of law. I've gone through Volume 1, Titles 1-6, statutes that make up Oregon's courts and Rules for Civil Procedure; Volume 2, Titles 7-9, business organizations; Volume 3, Titles 10-13, landlord-tenant, probate and domestic relations; and I'm currently studying Volume 4, Titles 14-16, crimes and criminal procedures.

Titles are again divided by chapters, which are subdivided by sections. The statutes are used as primary references and arguing points. When drafting petitions, motions, responses, etc., lawyers also use Opinions, Oregon Administrative Rules (OARs) and comparable cases to persuade the judge to grant their request.

The world of law is entirely made up of arbitrary terms, phrases that might have made sense at one point but hardly serve a purpose anymore, especially for people incarcerated. People make up the rules (promulgated through legislature) and then use those rules as an excuse to say they can't change the rules, because the rules say so.

It's a merciless system seemingly designed to keep those with power in power and those on the fringes of society on the fringes. Often, the statutes refer to themselves in such a convoluted manner it's hard to tell where one begins and another ends, like a worm eating itself. The whole thing makes me dizzy.

But things are not in a vacuum. Just as violence is not in a vacuum, pain, hurt, and injustice are not separate. Injustice doesn't become justice because a law says it does. Injustice is injustice regardless of people's opinions about it. Injustice is something you can feel in your bones. You instinctually know when something is unjust.

I once watched a Black inmate get in a fight with a White inmate. I watched as several COs broke up the fight with pepper spray. I watched as both men were detained and handcuffed by the COs. Then I watched two of the guards' kick and punch the Black guy after he had already been detained and handcuffed — the White guy just sat and watched. Like I said, you feel it in your bones. The Black guy was dragged off to the hole, and the White guy was shipped out to another prison. (I'm not sure if he went to the hole there or not.)

A few years ago, solitary confinement (the hole) started getting a bad rap around town, so they just changed the name. In Oregon, they call it "DSU" (Disciplinary Segregation Unit), "Ad-Seg" (Administrative Segregation), or "IMU" (Intensive

Management Unit). But it's all different words to disguise the same thing — the hole is the hole regardless of what you call it. It's a place where inmates are kept locked up in a six-by-nine-foot cell for sometimes months at a time by themselves. In Oregon the maximum is 180 days, which is still a lot, but there are loopholes that can keep inmates in solitary confinement a lot longer. Sometimes, inmates are shuffled between Ad-Seg, IMU, and DSU as a way of starting the "180-day clock" over.

OARs are rules that state agencies must follow. They are designed to keep agencies in line by following the ORS enacted by legislature. Ideally, the administrative rules should coincide with ORS... *ideally*. Because it is a state agency, the Department of Corrections (DOC) is governed by OARs (OAR 213, OAR 255, and OAR 291). The crimes committed by the defendant, however, are governed by state laws and, therefore, fall under ORS.

Sometimes the ORS and OARs aren't as transparent with each other as they should be. An inmate can be sentenced by a judge based upon statutes that aren't necessarily honored by the DOC. For example, a judge might agree to a plea deal accepted by both the defendant and the District Attorney (DA) with language in the judgment stating the defendant is eligible for good time served. In other words, if the defendant doesn't get into trouble in prison, he can have a reduction in his overall sentence.

The inmate agrees to the plea deal under the presumption he is eligible for up to twenty percent off his sentence (as agreed upon by the judge and the DA). But when the defendant gets to prison, the DOC says he's not eligible for good time based upon their own policies, which are based upon what some administrative rule says — a rule the judge might have not been familiar with at the time of sentencing. This often happens because the judge was agreeing to terms based upon statute and wasn't familiar with DOC rules and regulations. In return, the DOC will argue it doesn't have to honor a judgment if the judgment doesn't coincide with their policy and rules. A judge will blame the defense attorney for not representing his client better, a DA will say it's not their problem, and the defense attorney will say he has too many other clients and that the defendant should take it up on appeal. It's not about figuring out who to blame because, in the end, it only effects one person – the person in prison. Essentially, the defendant is screwed. He agreed to one outcome and got dealt another. The whole thing feels slimy, unethical, and also, par for the course. I've seen this happen dozens of times.

Figuring out how the whole thing works is a lot like trying to unscramble scrambled eggs, and unscrambling eggs is precisely the task I've taken on as the new jailhouse lawyer.

I'm allowed to bring two notebooks and pens to the law library, but I'm searched upon coming and going. I am not allowed to bring my radio, but they have a small radio in the law library that I can use from time to time. My parents sent me an old moleskin journal to write my notes in, which had to be pre-approved and checked thoroughly by the prison administration. (I used the same moleskin journals in college, so there's a nostalgia to writing notes like this.) When I'm in the law library, I can pretend I'm somewhere else, like a small café, albeit the worst café ever.

I'm also allowed coffee in the law library as long as I bring it up from my bunk. We only get powdered instacoffee here. It's expensive and shitty, but it's better than nothing. I remind myself that in prison it's all about the small luxuries — like squeeze cheese.

I sit down at my desk in the law library on a broken computer chair that doesn't like to cooperate. It tends to squeak and turn at odd times. I hate it. Fans and buzzing sounds go on randomly and make it hard to study, but I try to power through the intercoms, alarms, and buzzes as much as I can. It's better than the snoring.

I open a few books on statutes and administrative rules and begin to flip the pages, skimming through sections on crimes. I come across a section on burglary:

OAR 213-004-0010 - Burglary I

(1) A prior Burglary I (ORS 164.225 (Burglary in the first degree)) conviction for an offense committed after the effective date of these rules shall be classified for criminal history:

(a) As a prior person felony if that prior conviction was classified as a Crime Category 9 or 8 offense on the Crime Seriousness Scale (OAR 213-018-0025(1) and (2)); and

(b) As a prior non-person felony if that prior conviction was classified as a Crime Category 7 offense on the Crime Seriousness Scale (OAR 213-018-0025(3)).

(2) A prior Burglary I (ORS 164.225) conviction for an offense committed before the effective date of these rules or any juvenile adjudication for conduct, committed before or after the

effective date of these rules, which if committed by an adult would have constituted Burglary I shall be classified as a prior person felony if the State proves by a preponderance of the evidence that the criminal conduct would have been classified as a Crime Category 9 or 8 offense on the Crime Seriousness Scale (OAR 213-018-0025(1) and (2)), however if the State does not meet that burden of proof, then the prior offense shall be classified as a prior non-person felony in crime category 7 (213-018-0025(3)).

I write down what I can, taking note of the convolution between OAR and ORS and how they are oddly interwoven. I try to apply the statutes and laws in ways that might apply to situations here in prison. For example, the DA might take the administrative rule above and use it to try to persuade the judge to increase the defendant's sentence based upon a prior record, even if that crime took place a long time ago and was irrelevant to his current sentence. To put it plainly, the DA is trying to make someone's life, who is already miserable, a whole lot worse.

I write this down in my notebook so that I don't forget it. When I take notes, I remind myself of the blatant contrast between the sentencing laws and the inmates subject to those laws. Many of the inmates can't even read let alone try to navigate their way through their own legal troubles. Not too long ago, I saw an inmate reading a Dr. Seuss book in the dorm; he gave up halfway through and tossed the book against the wall.

I look at my example written down in my journal. It makes me feel alone. This country no longer represents its people. We are just poor statistics and numbers. We are votes. The men who put us away have no idea who we are, but I realize too that they have no idea who they are either — lions at night, and mice in the morning. They don't realize their roars only project a profound loneliness within themselves. The deeper connection in meditation reminds me that no action is in isolation. I wonder if the people who put us away go to sleep at night realizing that, in putting us away, they are putting themselves away too.

I feel the paper of my journal within my fingers, and I smile. I smile at the feeling my hand gets when I write or when I figure something out. I smile at the fresh ink on the page, the way it lays softly on the thick journal paper. I smile at the black ink that comes jetting out of the tip of the gel pen. Black ink is considered contraband in prison because the inmates use it for stick and poke tattoos. (All you need is some black ink, a few guitar strings, and voilà — freshly painted swastikas.) I'm only permitted black ink in the law library for legal documents. I have to turn in the pens before I go back down to the dorm.

I look back at my notes trying to pierce it into my memory. I try to think about both sides. I try to put it into perspective. The DA just thinks he's doing his or her job. Maybe she's getting her numbers, or he's meeting his quota. Maybe the DA isn't in a good marriage. Maybe they fill their time with work. Maybe this case is the case that determines whether or not they get re-elected come November. It's all possible. But then I think about the other side: the reality is that just a simple request could mean the difference of ten years. That's ten years someone is away from their children, ten years away from their spouse, ten years away from the smell of free air, and real cheese.

Many statistics show that rehabilitation after ten years

is nearly impossible. All for a burglary? I wonder (and this is not to condone burglary at all), what is the price to see a person as a human being? After all, maybe he was just laid off. Maybe gas is now $5.00 a gallon and he can't afford to commute to his job. Or maybe he can't find a job at all because he's a felon; nobody hires felons, so he's forced to burglarize homes to feed his kids. Ten extra years? Seriously? I can't stomach it. I feel like DAs, prosecutors, and maybe even judges should all spend one month in prison just to know what they're sending these men and women to.

The laws are written like stone, but they are not made of stone. They are made by people. They bend and break and twist (for those who can afford it).

But what do I know, I've never been to law school; I'm just a jail house lawyer. It has given me a little bit of street cred but not much. Some of the inmates call me Saul Goodman (from Breaking Bad and Better Call Saul), but most of them still call me Muhammad or worse.

I spend the afternoon writing down notes, reading, sipping on powdered coffee, and every once in a while, twisting around in my chair. The law library continues to buzz with intercom noises, alarms, and radios going off in the distance, but I'm alone — what a weird thing to process. I'm alone. The solitude is uncomfortable and comfortable at the same time, like finding an old, itchy wool sweater you thought you'd lost. The solitude feels like a cave within me or a heavy blanket pulled over me. I'm grateful to be alone, but I know in just a few hours, I'll be back down with all the other inmates. It's like being taken to the ocean, but not being allowed to touch the water.

After a few hours of studying, I close my notebook and sit back in my chair, trying to ignore the squeaking. I reach up and grab the radio from a shelf above the computer. I plug it in and turn it on. The 12:00 a.m. red lights begin to blink on and off. I push the snooze buttons a few times, and a few other buttons until I figure out how to change the frequency (a small button with a plus sign on the side of the radio). I click it, and a blast of static comes blaring through the speakers — perfect.

I sit back in my chair and wait a few moments. Every hour a guard comes in and checks on me, writes the time on a clipboard, initials it, looks around the room, and then leaves. I'm just a few minutes from the next check, and I don't want to be written up for "not working."

Like clockwork, the guard comes marching in, acknowledges me for a moment, signs the clipboard, and then walks out of the room. I've got sixty minutes until he comes back. I figure I've earned a twenty-minute meditation break after studying for almost three hours straight.

I turn up the static on the radio and close my eyes.

I breathe in with the sound. It smells different in the law library. It's hard to get used to the smell. I open my eyes and look out the window, but there are no trees. There is just an empty room with concrete floors and stacked tables and chairs. The lights are fluorescent and buzzing. This building is like a Home Depot if Home Depot had nothing in it. I can tell my body craves something natural. My body craves an earth that it no longer feels a part of.

I invite the light within me. I invite a divinity to open me up to something larger. I first open up by acknowledging the little I have. I am grateful for this space. I am grateful for my health. I am grateful for my body — my Brown body. I am grateful for my parents. I am grateful for the land and sun, and the ocean in the distance. I imagine myself there, standing on the shore, looking out at her waves. I breathe in the white noise. I smile because I no longer have to hold the headphones over my ears.

I can feel the waves creep up around my ankles. I'm not wearing jeans — no denim, thank God. I'm in shorts, my feet are free from any boots or prison shoes. My toes make an impression in the sand as they begin to sink below the beachy surface. The water rises up now to my shins. The tide must be coming in. At first, the water feels cold, not numbing cold, just cold enough to notice, but after some time, I barely feel it.

I watch as the waves come in around me, encircling me and holding me. When I breathe in, the waves come in. When I breathe out, the waves go out. My body and its breath have amalgamated with the sea. After ten or so inhales and exhales the ocean is up to my waist. I can't tell if I am walking out to meet her, or if she is coming in to meet me. I am not afraid. I welcome her like an old friend.

After my twentieth inhale, my whole body is underwater. It is peaceful and calm. I allow my body the space to just float calmly in the water. There is a sound to peace. There is a sound to stillness. It's the sound of being underwater alone, with nothing to distract me. I begin to see my thoughts. I can see each one represented by a different color. I can feel the anger in me — red. I see the red rising up my arm. I brush some of it off into the water. I watch as the red dye of anger bleeds into the ocean. I take a deeper inhale. Then I notice green — separation, or distance from the earth. I can feel it in my chest area. I begin to rub some of the green around my chest, smearing it in a circle like chalk. The green begins to melt in me, not off of my body like the red. I stand here underwater doing this with all the colors. I rub blues, purples, yellows, and oranges. One by one, each color melts into me and then burns off into the ocean water. I can feel the static from the law library radio intensify and thicken, the volume begins to burgeon louder in the room.

Deep in this ocean, I watch as the colors wash off one by one. I watch the colors float below to my feet and then seep into the wet sand. I stand here underwater motionless for some time. I feel the hurt, but I don't know what to do with it. I feel the anger, and I don't know what to do with that either. Suddenly, small little green stems begin to sprout out of the sand where the colors went. I watch them slowly grow longer until they begin to grow little petals and bloom little yellow flowers. I don't know the flowers, it's hard to see them in the water. It's like looking out of a car windshield in the rain without the wipers turned on. I'm not sure what the flowers mean, but it doesn't matter…I open my eyes. There's an inmate here to see me.

The inmate is standing in the doorway with the guard. He has a half-broken pencil and an old pad of notebook paper in his hand, along with some folded up legal documents. His head is clean-shaven and bald with the numbers 88 tattooed behind his ears and on his elbows. He's AB, or Aryan Brotherhood. The 88 is a common tattoo here. It represents the 8th letter in the alphabet: HH (Hail Hitler).

The man sits down begrudgingly. I turn off the radio.

"I don't want him to help me," the inmate says to the guard.

"It doesn't look like you have a choice, does it? He's the legal beagle after all," the guard replies sternly. "If you don't want help, I can take you back to your bunk."

I watch the inmate contemplate it for a while, before he reluctantly mutters, "Fine."

I close the door, but the guard sits outside in a chair. I'm sure the Lieutenant told him to stay close, just in case.

The inmate stares at me for a while, and I just stare back.

"We can sit here for sixty minutes and do nothing, or I can help you," I finally say to him.

"Don't fucking talk to me," the inmate replies.

"Look man," I say to him. "I can either help you with your legal problems, or you can leave. I don't really care."

We sit for ten minutes in silence, which is fine… I like the silence.

"My bitch is filing for divorce," the man finally mutters.

"I'm sorry, I didn't hear you."

"I said, my bitch is filing for divorce," the man yells at me angrily.

"I'm sorry to hear that. Let me see what you've got."

I grab the legal papers from his hands and look at the documents. I read the first page. "Petitioner's Petition for Dissolution of Marriage." He's been served.

"Divorce. I'm sorry. That must be tough. What do you want to do about it?" I ask him.

"I don't fucking care. She's not getting my truck, that's for damn sure."

"She will if you don't respond within thirty days," I reply.

"What?" the inmate asks me.

"It's a law in Oregon that the Respondent, that's you, has to file an answer within thirty days or the Petitioner can win by default."

"Even if I'm in prison?" the man asks.

"Yeah, I don't think it matters. You've got to respond, and it looks like you received this document..." I shuffle through the pages. "Two weeks ago, which gives you about two weeks to get a response written, out the door, and received by the courts...otherwise she *can* take your truck."

"That's fucked up."

I don't say anything. There's a lull of silence before I ask him, "Do you have any kids?"

"What the fuck you care?" the man responds angrily.

"Well, are you going to want to file for custody? Split custody? We should probably include that in your response."

"She already has full custody."

The inmate and I slowly go through the documents one by one, filling out the necessary items. I write out his answers and responses, line by line, and draft a document: "Respondent's Response to Petitioners Petition for Dissolution of Marriage." It's a mouthful.

When the hour is up, I tell him to come up to see me tomorrow so we can get this out the door. He gets up and walks out without saying a word.

The next day, the inmate shows up at the law library at

8 a.m. We continue to work through the necessary papers, and I show him the draft he needs to sign.

"We need to sign it and send it out certified mail," I tell him.

"What does that mean?" he asks.

"We need to show the courts that we responded to her and show proof of service."

I pull open a page in the back of a book on Oregon Rules for Civil Procedures (ORCP).

"ORCP 7 is all about how to serve documents properly. We have to show the courts proof of service that your wife, or ex-wife now, received the documents that we filed with the court. Otherwise, it goes into default, which means that your ex-wife would automatically get everything."

"I don't care about the laws. I'll just do what you tell me I need to do."

"It's your call. It's a lot of work and will cost you money, but in the end, it might save you a lot of money too."

I watch the man closely. It's a precarious situation. He's at least a foot taller than me, has a hundred pounds over me, and could probably put me in a coma with a single swing. He rides with the Whites and is openly a Nazi sympathizer. He's called me terrible things and pushed me into bunks before, but now, sitting here in this room, he's in need of my help. I have the power here, and he knows it. I could steer this guy in the wrong direction, and he could lose everything. After all, he deserves it. Who's to say his wife doesn't deserve to take everything of his, even his truck? I don't blame her. Maybe he beats her. Maybe she is trying to protect the kids. I'm not sure I have much compassion for Nazi sympathizers and racists.

I consider the consequences. The thoughts race through my mind but only for a moment because, in the end,

I know I am going to help him. It's the right thing to do. Resentment is a lot like passing a slow car on the highway just to come upon another slow car —with resentment, there is always another car.

"Think on it, and let me know what you want to do," I tell him.

He looks down at the divorce papers. I watch him carefully. I see how he hunches his shoulders. I see how he ruffles the pages between his fingers. I can tell he doesn't want them to be real. When he's down with the other inmates, he stands up tall and puffs his chest like a rooster, but in here, he's wobbly and hunched over. This White supremacist of a man is like all the other White supremacists in here: broken, scared, tired, and angry. Men in here, even the worst of men, are just kids in adult bodies. They live by a code they were taught when they were young, and their parents were probably taught the same code: Be a man, and hate everyone who does not look and think like you. I look at this kid across from me, and I can see the truth. He has no idea who he is. He already has nothing, and he's about to lose even more. The least I can do is try to help him.

We fill out all the paperwork and put the necessary postage on to get it to the right place.

"Sign here, and then you need to fill out the address here," I tell him.

He hesitates. This usually means the man doesn't have a signature.

"Do you know how to write your signature?" I ask him gently.

"Not really," the man admits hesitantly.

"Okay, just scribble something here."

The man does as I tell him.

There's a real deepening of light happening. I can feel it in me. What an odd situation I find myself in — helping my oppressor. A part of me knows that his ex-wife is probably better off. A part of me knows nothing is going to change with this man. In here, up in this room, away from all the inmates, he'll talk to me because he needs me to help him, but I know, as soon as we get back down to the main part of the prison, I will be his enemy again. He won't change.

I don't know this man's story. I can only guess, but a lot of it is the same. Underneath this giant meat suit, splattered in swastikas and prison ink, there's a person — a wounded energy desperately looking for healing.

We finish the documents and seal them.

"That's it?" he asks.

"That's it."

"Okay," the man says.

He doesn't smile or say "Thank you." He nods. It's all he can do.

We step outside and wait for the guard to come and get us. It's warm and bright outside the law library. The sun peers through the clouds. I can feel the warmth seep into my clothes and tighten my skin. I glance up at the clouds; gigantic foams of omnibus swirl and dance across the blue sky above me. There's a slight breeze. I can feel it against my hair, which is tied up in its usual bun. The pavement beneath our feet soaks in the sun and makes everything hot. I look around, nothing but concrete and rocks.

Then I see small little green sprouts in the cracks of the

concrete. A sign of earth trying to break through. I notice small little yellow flowers popping up out of the pavement, pushing their way through stone. I walk over to one of the cracks and bend down near the flower. The petals are bright yellow, with a large brown puffball center. I've seen these flowers before. They're some of the only flowers down in the yard. They push through everything.

"Brown-Eyed Susans," the man says from afar.

I turn around.

"What's that?" I ask him.

"They're Brown-Eyed Susans." he says again. He pauses. "We get those flowers a lot. They're stubborn. They grow through everything. Concrete. Rocks. They're tough, resilient mother fuckers."

I look at the man curiously, but I don't say anything. I just smile.

"My wife gardens… well, ex-wife."

It's the last thing he says to me.

I pick one of the Brown-Eyed Susans and place it between the pages in my moleskin journal. After a few minutes, the guard shows up to take us back down to the dorm. We go through two gates that buzz, showing our IDs on the way.

When we get back down to the main part of the prison, the man doesn't say anything to me. He doesn't smile or acknowledge me; he just walks off. I know that he won't ever say anything to me again. Odds are, he'll probably still call me names and shake my bunk as he walks by — which he does.

There's a code here in prison, just like there's a code out there. It's an us vs. them code that lives and breathes and takes on a whole life in here, as it does out there. It covers our culture like concrete over the earth. It blankets the healing with unhealing. The codes of prison are the codes everywhere else.

Like statutes and administrative rules, these codes have never represented the real need. They symbolize an unheard and unhealed humanity. My body is showing me that there is an energy underneath, a resilient and enduring energy, waiting to be tapped into.

I get back to my bunk to put my things away, but before doing so, I open my journal, take out the Brown-Eyed Susan, and put her on my bookshelf next to my radio.

Chapter Eleven

Smoke Signals

I am beginning to feel parts of my body that I wasn't aware of before. My body is my greatest teacher, and I am learning to listen to him in new ways. When I breathe in, I can feel the signals. My body sends energy where it needs to go, but some of the energy feels trapped, occluded by hurt, thwarted by something, in some distant time. I don't know how to heal those parts. I feel the energy push against the walls, but there is no budging.

When I meditate and center myself, a calm wave of light washes over me. In this concrete jungle, I feel the displacement. My body yearns for earth. It yearns for soil, grass, forests, and mountains. In this meditative light, I can feel those places I long for, just as I feel the different parts of my body, like my kidneys, my stomach, or my heart. Am I connected to the earth in a much deeper way? Can I go there?

I plug in the radio in the law library. I've been studying for a few hours, and I need a break. The red 12:00 a.m. lights blink on and off. I turn the radio to a cool static, a gentler rain. I lean back in my squeaky computer chair and rest my hands over my lap. The silence is like entering a cool cave underwater, the soundlessness echoing off the ancient cavern walls of my body. Here, I can drown out the prison alarms and buzzes and intercoms. In this silence, everything becomes distant. When I close my eyes, I feel like I can go anywhere.

I begin to travel deeper into my own body, following a

light somewhere down within my being. The light is not psychedelic or flashy. It is not new age or pseudo-spiritual. It's a gentle light, like looking up and seeing the sun from underneath the water. It beats warmly not intensely. As I follow the light inward, I can feel parts of my body twitch — often my fingers or my legs. I am aware of the sensations. It's a similar twitch I get during acupuncture. The muscles twitch to relax and release energy. My meditation seems to be doing the same thing naturally.

Slowly, the gentle light becomes a winter green. I can feel myself being pulled into a field. The static becomes a gentle rain. I look around: it is just a large, grassy field, but I am not alone. I am with my younger self, but he looks quite a bit older now — maybe twenty? This is not a memory. I have never been to this field, but here I am with my twenty-year-old self now, here, in some real moment, in some real body. He sees me. I think he knows me now, at least a little bit.

He is wearing a brown flannel, black jeans, a beanie, and a Patagonia coat — very PNW of him. His hair is long and curly, but he wears it to one side. He's skinnier still. He's young, and he doesn't have prison strength yet. He has a small yin-yang necklace around his neck, and his black jeans are rolled up slightly at the ankles. He has brown thick-rimmed Ray-Ban glasses. He's not as cautious as my thirteen-year-old self. He's more confident, friendly, and conversational. In just seven years, he's become a master at blending in. He knows exactly what he needs to do to hide his emotions. He looks at me and smiles; I feel a twitch in my leg.

"Nice getup," he jokes, pointing to my prison clothes. Still getting dissed by a younger me. Perfect.

"You too," I jest back, pointing to his brown thick-rimmed Ray-Bans.

"Touché," he replies.

The rain is still falling, only so much that we feel it on our hands and faces, but our clothes don't feel wet. The field is green, like really green — Oregon green. There are a few scattered fir and pine trees in the distance, but the space is open and expansive.

"I've never been here before," I say to my twenty-year-old self.

"Neither have I," he returns.

"Do you know where we are?" I ask.

"I thought you would know," he responds.

It's a very odd feeling. I know that I am still in my body in the law library, fully aware, but this meditation brings me somewhere else. I feel like I am in two places at once. I feel another twitch in my leg.

"Do you know who I am?" I ask him.

Dumb question, I think to myself.

"Dumb question," he says simultaneously, almost as if he's reading my mind.

I'm half expecting him to say something profound. I'm half expecting him to lead me inward and show me something, like a vision, but this doesn't happen. We just stand in this field together. I look up at the falling rain, the white noise steadily rumbling from the law library radio, and then back at my younger self.

"Let's build a fire," I say to him.

I don't know where the idea comes from, but it feels right.

"Okay," he responds.

We begin to gather small sticks from the field. I'm not sure if they were there before, but they are appearing as we need them, as I need them, as my body needs them — another twitch. After a few moments, we meet back in the middle of the field and begin to build a small fire. The grass is not long, and the rain is steady enough now that we're not afraid of burning the field. The sky is overcast and gray.

"Feels like fall," I tell my younger self.

"Must be," he replies.

We stack the sticks against each other like a teepee. I watch my younger self pull out a Bic lighter from his coat pocket and hand it to me.

"Wanna do the honors?" he asks.

I take the lighter and crouch down to the ground, one hand in the soil, the other on the lighter, and flip the clicker back. It feels a lot like the dial on my radio. Though it's raining, the sticks have no problem lighting.

We watch as the flames quickly rise. They aren't out of control, but we need more wood. We walk around the field, this time finding much larger logs and branches. We come back to the fire and place the larger branches around the sticks.

We stand silently for a few moments, just watching the flames rise in the rain. They are bright orange and stand out against the gray, overcast sky. We watch the smoke billow upward from the fire, swirling around in a spiral. My younger self grabs a medium-size stick from the fire and begins to twirl it around in circles.

"Smoke signals," he says to me.

"Who are we trying to signal?" I ask him curiously. Somehow, I have an idea.

I watch silently as my younger self twirls the stick in circles with his wrist, sending out the smoke signals to the far reaches of the Universe. I can see the orange glow of the fire bouncing off his yin-yang necklace. I know this version of myself, I think to myself. This is a young me in search of many answers, answers that may not come for another decade, or more.

Then, out of nowhere, we see an old woman walk into the field. She has long, smooth, gray hair wrapped in a ponytail. Her eyes are green and gentle. She is also wearing a flannel and jeans, but she's barefoot. She is carrying a backpack slung over one shoulder. The skin under her eyes is wrinkled and worn by time, but she does not look weary. She wears a warm smile.

"Sorry I'm late," she says to us. "Traffic."

She sets her bag down between us and turns toward my younger self.

"Looking for me?" she asks him.

My younger self turns to me, hoping I'll answer for the both of us.

"I'm not sure," I pause. "Who are you?"

My younger self stays quiet, and the woman smiles warmly.

"Please, sit," she replies.

We sit down in the grass next to the fire. Immediately, my jeans get soaked from the wet ground. The static of rain continues to steadily fall on us from above. (Glad to know the radio is still working.)

We sit and stare into the fire for some time. All of us remain quiet, not needing to talk. We just watch the flames glow upward, the wood sometimes crackling with a spark.

Finally, the woman turns to my twenty-year-old self.

"You feel distant," she says.

I can't tell if it's a question or a statement. It's non-threatening though; it's tender and soft. I'm not sure what she means by it; somehow my body knows though. In the end, it's not me that answers.

"Yes," my younger self responds.

The woman smiles.

"You don't have to feel distant," she returns, in a matter-of-fact manner.

I look over at my younger self, curious to see how he'll respond. I am a bystander now, an observer. I watch the two converse back and forth. Somehow, I think he knows what's going on. Somehow, I think he needs this more than I do. I feel another twitch in my leg.

"Take off your shoes," she says to him.

He takes shoes off and then his socks, folding them up and shoving them into his shoes to keep them dry.

"How do your feet feel now?" she asks.

He places them firmly into the grass.

"Better," he says.

"Not as distant?"

"No," he answers.

"It's important not to feel so closed off from the land that grounds us," she says. "The earth grounds us. It's important to stay connected to her."

My younger self knows exactly what she means. I do too.

"But I'm not sure I know what I am looking for," he says.

"Why?" she asks him.

"I don't know. I'm not sure," he responds.

I watch the smoke continue to rise from the fire. I follow it up into the air until it gets lost in the gray.

"Why are you looking for something else? Maybe it is already here," the woman says, looking around the field and then up into the sky.

"I don't know. I think I'm looking for something different," my younger self replies to her cautiously.

I watch the woman pull out a Nalgene water bottle from her backpack, unscrew the cap, and take a large gulp of water.

"Ahhhh," she says loudly, after swallowing a gulp. "That's better."

Then she reaches into her backpack and pulls out a small branch of cedar.

"For healing and cleansing," she says.

She lights the cedar and lets the needles crackle a moment before blowing it out. Immediately, the smell of burnt cedar rises from the branch. It is the smell of earth. It is the smell of the land purifying.

"It is her gift to us. Be grateful, and let it heal you."

I watch my younger self take in a huge inhale of Cedar. I watch as he breathes the earth in a new way. His body begins to feel lighter, and simultaneously, my body begins to feel lighter. There is another twitch in my leg. I feel some old energy being released.

I watch my younger self carefully. I can tell he feels guilty. The woman knows it too.

"Why do you feel guilty?" she asks.

"Because…" he answers, "this makes more sense to me."

"Hasn't it always?" she asks.

He doesn't answer.

There is a sadness in his eyes. There is a sadness in her eyes too. He wants so badly to be a part of something that he knows he'll feel guilty for. He's not ready. I know this, because I remember being twenty and not being ready. The woman walks over to my younger self and crouches down. She takes his hand gently in hers.

"Soon," she says. "Not yet, but soon."

Then the woman is gone. My younger self and I are left in the field, standing in the rain and smoke.

There is a knock at the door. I open my eyes, and I'm back in the law library. I twist around in the chair and see Smalls standing in the doorway.

"What's up, Li'l Mod? I need your help," he says to me.

Smalls plops down in the chair opposite of me. I look like a child, sitting next to his big, Black body.

"How are you?" I ask.

"You know, you know. Them motherfuckers can't keep me down. Listen…" he continues, "first they fuckin' steal my property — photos of my wife. Then, they put me in the hole, no warning — nothing. And, when I got out, some of my shit was missing. Anything you can do?"

"What was missing?" I asked.

"My radio. Photos. My remote for my TV. Snacks. A bunch of shit. I know it was that CO."

"The one who arrested you?"

"Yeah, man, that man is dirty. No good if you ask me," Smalls says, shaking his head. "We're like honeybees in this jar, feel me?"

"Let me see what I can do," I respond.

I twist back in my chair and pull out a few books on administrative rules, in particular OAR 213 and 291, the agency rules for Prison.

"Smalls," I say to him. "Do you have your papers?"

Papers is a term used in prison to refer to someone's

judgment. A judgment is a formal legal document that lists your crime, the sentencing, the post-prison supervision, where you fall on the grid, how much money you owe the courts, etc. It's not a good thing to ask to see someone's papers in prison — it's politics — but being in the law-library, it's different. I am asking him for legal reasons.

He pulls out his judgment and hands it me. I read the charges and crime severity.

"Give me a few minutes," I say to him.

"Take your time, Li'l Mod," he responds as he slouches back in his chair. "I got nowhere to go," he chuckles.

After twenty minutes of reading through statutes and rules, I stop and pause.

"Hey, Smalls," I say to him, still looking down at the laws.

"What's up?" he answers.

"Were you ever arrested? Like… before this time?"

"No," he says.

"Never convicted before, never had a felony, nothing? You don't have any other charges?"

"Nothing," Smalls replies. I look down at this judgment and then back down at the papers.

"I might have found something, but I need to be sure," I say cautiously.

"What's that? Some rules about COs taking my shit?" he asks.

"Bigger," I respond.

I look down at his judgment. I read the words "Class C Felony."

"Class C?" I ask him.

"Yes," he responds.

In Oregon, there are three types of felonies: Class A,

B, and C. Class A is the most serious of felonies, holding a maximum sentencing of up to twenty years in prison. Class C has a maximum of five years.

"Pursuant to ORS 161.605, a Class C felony has a maximum sentence of up to five years," I say to Smalls.

"Pursuant a-what-now?" Smalls replies confused.

"How many charges were you convicted of total?" I ask him.

"Two," he responds.

"Consecutive or concurrent?"

"I dunno what that means, Li'l Man," Smalls replies.

"Consecutive means you are serving sentence time one after the other for each charge. Concurrent means together. Like for example, if you got charged with two crimes and both were Class C felonies and consecutive, that would mean you'd be serving potentially ten years, right? Up to five years for the first felony charge, and up to five years for the second felony charge."

"Right, I follow."

"But," I continue, "if you were charged concurrently, that means the sentences for each charge run together at the same time…Meaning, five years maximum, regardless of the number of charges. If the judge said it was a concurrent sentence, even if you had ten charges, the most you could serve is five years. Now," I continue. "I'm not a lawyer. I've never been to law school. I'm doing my best and kind of winging it here, but I think I'm reading the statutes correctly."

"Right," Smalls answers. "I think it was concurrent, but I don't know."

"Oddly enough, your judgment doesn't say whether it's concurrent or not, but it should."

"It's supposed to?" he asks.

"Yes."

"Does that mean they fucked up? Like I could get out or some shit."

"No, you can't get out just because they messed up on the judgment. They call that a clerical error, which is not an error apparent on the face of the record, or an error of law. What I mean is, clerical errors are not enough to get someone out of prison. If there is a clerical error on a judgment, the court can just fix the judgement to reflect the actual sentencing. But, if I am reading this correctly, it might be more than just a clerical error. It looks like you were given 392 days credit for time served, is that correct?"

"I'm not sure, Li'l Man, but I'm listening now. What you getting at?" Smalls responds.

"ORS 137.320, subsection 4, says that the sheriff of the county jail must compute the time you were in jail before you were convicted. That time must then be credited toward your overall sentence."

"What does that mean exactly?" Smalls asks me.

"Well, you were arrested more than five years ago. You were sentenced less than four years ago, but you spent over a year in county jail waiting for your sentence. This means that if you were given concurrent sentences, the maximum you could face for a Class C felony is…"

"Five years," Smalls interjects.

"That's right," I respond. "Five years total, including the time you served in county. Considering you served 392 days in county, if you were given concurrent sentencing…" I pull out a calculator and begin to push in some buttons. "It means, you've served already, including time in jail, 1,929 days. The maximum for a Class C Felony, 5 years, 365 days x 5 equals 1,825. That would mean, you're 104 days over."

"Over sentenced? Hell, no!" Smalls shouts.

"Well, I mean, we'd have to check to make sure you were sentenced concurrently on these two charges and not consecutively, but ideally, yeah, it's possible."

"They fucked up."

"Potentially," I respond. "We need to write a letter to the court and ask for a judgment with the right language or even write a Motion for a Modification of Judgment. We need clear language stating whether or not your sentence was concurrent or consecutive, and we need to see clear language stating you get credit for time served in the amount of 392 days. I can't promise anything, but it's worth a shot."

"Alright, Li'l Mod," Smalls says excitedly. "Let's do it."

Two weeks later, I call Smalls up to the law library. The court has responded to the request for a modified judgment.

Smalls sits down in the chair and opens the envelope. I can tell he's nervous.

"It's all good," I tell him. He opens the judgment and begins to read it quickly, scanning the pages nervously.

"I dunno how to read this, Li'l Man," Smalls says to me.

"Want me to look?" I ask him.

"Yeah."

I grab the judgment from him and the turn the pages over. I spot it immediately.

"Concurrent," I tell him, succinctly. "Credit for time served."

"Concurrent?" he asks.

"Concurrent," I respond.

"That's good, right?"

"Yeah, I mean… I think you are being illegally detained."

I hold my composure well, but inside, I'm shocked. I think the DOC might have just screwed this guy over.

"I'm not a lawyer, so I can't make any promises," I say, "but yeah, this looks promising, man. You weren't given your credit for time served. We need to write the court immediately. I'm not sure in what form… maybe a letter? Maybe a Motion for Immediate Release from Custody of DOC. We also need to tell the DOC, but they're all kinds of fucked up and probably wouldn't take you seriously without a response from a judge first. So, let's start there."

"Okay, Li'l Man," Smalls answers with optimism. "Let's start there."

It doesn't take long. Four days later, I'm called up to the administration building, and so is Smalls. When we get up to the building, the Lieutenant is waiting for both of us. He has a legal document folded in his hand.

"This is serious," he says, pointing down at the documents. I don't say anything back.

"Smalls," the Lt. continues, "you're going to be immediately released from prison… today. Go pack your things."

Smalls looks at me in shock, then at the Lt., and then back at me. He smiles, rushes up and hugs me. "Hell, yeah. Hell, yeah, man."

The Lt. stands stoically, but I can sense a smile underneath his blank face.

"Come to my office when you're done packing, both of you, please."

The Lt. walks off around the corner, and into the admin building.

Smalls turns to me.

"Thank you," he says.

"You're welcome," I respond. "Listen," I tell him. "I'm not a lawyer, so I'm not sure… but I think you could probably get a lot of money for being wrongfully detained. You'll want to hire a civil lawyer and look into wrongful detention. Might be a tort claim, but I'm not sure. I'd look into it immediately."

"Thank you. I will," Smalls says to me. "You know," he continues, "You're not too bad, Li'l Mod. You're a fucking smart cat. Don't tell anyone I told you that though," he says with a smile.

"I won't," I chuckle. "It's the least I could do."

"No, man. This is big," I watch Smalls pause and then look down at the dorm from atop the stairs. "Yeah, you're different. We all know it. People in here don't like different. But people out there don't like different either."

"I know," I tell him.

"Don't worry, though, Li'l Man. People out there don't like people like me either. They give both of us a rough time because they're scared of us, you know. As they should be, because we're dangerous," he says to me with a smile. "Just remember your day will come, you don't belong here either."

"I'm not sure any of us do," I reply.

Smalls smirks, raises his hands up over his shoulders and looks down at the yard in the distance.

"Man, this place, this place is a fucking jar! I ain't gonna miss it, nope." He turns back to me again. "Thank you, man, really."

He gives me one last pat on my back and then heads down to the dorm to pack his belongings.

I turn and walk inside to the admin building and into the Lt.'s office.

"Lieutenant," I say, "you wanted to see me?" I ask him.

"Sit please."

I do as he says. He stares stoically at me for some time. He hides his emotions well. He has a good poker face; I can't tell if we're playing chess or checkers.

Finally, the Lt. breaks the silence.

"Off the record...You did a good job, and you did a good thing for him."

"And on the record?" I ask.

"Nothing. That's it. Sometimes the DOC gets it wrong," he admits.

"Is that off the record too?" I ask.

He pauses, then he looks me in the eye...

"Sometimes the system gets it wrong, too."

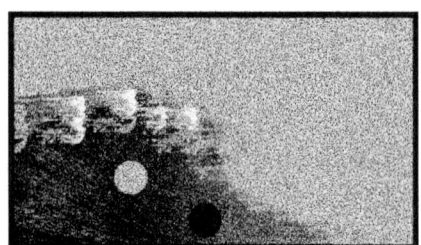

Meditation

My friends,

What if the Universe was for you?
What then would you do with your life?

In meditation, we learn acceptance. We learn to allow. We learn Wu Wei, which may take a lifetime (or several). In meditation, we learn how to notice and observe what is inside us, as well as what is all around us.

We also learn how to grieve and sit with sadness. In sitting with our own grief, we sit with the world's grief. It never fully goes away, but we learn to accept the grief within ourselves. We begin to see that it is not actually trying to hurt us. Our wound teaches us that we are more than the guilt and the shame. It shows us that we are part of a vast current, flowing alongside everything else, opening us up to endless possibilities. This kind of joy includes the wound. This kind of transformation does not exclude anything at all. In it, all paths lead us.

My friends,

Whether you believe it or not, the Universe is on your side, but you have to be on your side too! Being still with the earth and still with yourself will teach you to see the larger patterns of the Universe, which make up everything. The more we learn to discern these larger patterns, the less scary they become. The more time you spend with these larger patterns, the more you will begin to see the smaller spiritual patterns woven in between them.

It's these smaller spiritual patterns that make up who you are. When you come to the realization that you are not separate from the Universe, you will be able to shift these patterns within you ever so slightly and, therein, shift the energies of the Universe around you ever so slightly as well. This shifting is what leads to new perspectives: new perspectives on how you see the earth, how you see animals, how you see others, and how you see yourself.

It is true, there are so many injustices and so many wounds, and our system is entangled in all of it. While we are a part of this entangled system, we are not defined by it. The Universe is trying to show us that we are "both/and." But because we are stubborn and habitual in our routines and patterns, this can take time. Thankfully, the Universe is more patient than we are. She is gracious, and she responds accordingly to the energy we are able to receive.

We all carry a spiritual energy within us that has real effects on others around us, not just people but animals, the land, and, of course, ourselves. What we do in one part of our body effects another. The way we stand on our feet effects our posture, which effects our back and shoulders. Chi energy shows us that it's all connected in our body; and it's all connected everywhere else too.

Have you ever walked into a room and felt the anger and tension in the air? Maybe people were yelling or arguing. Maybe they had already stopped by the time you arrived. Yet, somehow, you could still feel the tension. This is all prison ever was — hot angry tension. I could feel it everywhere I went. I could just sense it; it's how I knew to get out of potentially dangerous situations. The more I became in tune with my body, the more I became aware of everything else. I began to notice the small, spiritual patterns within me, and I began to notice the small spiritual patterns in everyone else around me too. This didn't only help me to navigate the racism and violence, but it also helped me to discern and understand the men who came to me for legal help. Spiritual patterns can show us what we all have in common. When you are reading another, are you not just reading parts of yourself too?

Discerning the patterns within doesn't just help us navigate others, but it also helps us learn how to give of ourselves. Have you ever had a bad day where nothing seemed to go right, but then someone with a kind disposition did something for you and it changed the energy? Maybe they opened the door for you in passing, allowed you to cut in line, or bought your coffee for you. Maybe all they did was smile, but in that instant, that person had a power in them that changed the flow of energy within you, which changed the course of your day.

We have that same power within us to change the flow of energy for others. What we do with the spiritual energy inside of us has a lasting effect on other spiritual energies everywhere, because it's all a connected energy. The Universe can feel our energy, and she responds accordingly. The Divine knows us, often better than we know ourselves. When we are hard on ourselves or when we give into the habitual pattern of not feeling like we're enough, this energy is felt across the universe. The law of conservation of energy shows that energy is never created or destroyed but transformed. So where does the energy of our anger go? Where does the energy of our wounds go?

We cannot push it away.

It will only go somewhere else and hurt someone else.

So, we must transform it.

In so doing, we transform ourselves.

The way we see

Changing the way we see ourselves changes the way we see everything. I'd like to offer an exercise, but I must admit, it is not my own. The following meditation is my interpretation and expression of something passed down to me from a mentor. This exercise became very useful to me in prison, but it's not the easiest exercise to practice. So, go slow and be gentle. This could be an exercise that you practice over several months, or several lifetimes. It is something that I often have to return to for myself. It's a small way of changing how we see others around us, not as other, but as our very self.

First, find a quiet place. Still yourself and focus on your breathing.

Just allow and be with your breath.

I want you to picture someone you care for very dearly sitting across from you. This person should be someone that comes to mind easily. Maybe it's a spouse, partner, or best friend. I want you to picture them sitting across from you, and imagine they're feeling hurt. Imagine they are in pain. Imagine they have lost something or someone very dear to them. You love them, and you feel sorry for them. So you want to help, but nothing you can do will help them. The only thing you can do is just be present for them as they need it:

How do they hurt?

Can you feel their hurt?

What does their pain feel like?

Does it feel like your pain, or does it feel like something else?

Tell this person that you love them, and you care for them.

How does that make you feel?

How does that make them feel?

Can you become their pain? Can you become their loss and their hurt?

Over time, has your love helped them at all?

Has it helped you?

It is very important to notice the energy. Notice the resistance (if there is any) and notice the openness you feel when going through these questions.

Is there a pulling or tightening in your body?

Is there a loosening when you respond to certain questions?

In this exercise, we learn to feel the hurt and the wound of someone we love very dearly. We learn to sit with this pain. In sitting with it, we learn to feel the slight energy shifts of what it means to carry another beside yourself. But we are not done.

After a couple days, I want you to repeat the same exercise above, but this time I want you to think of someone not so special to you. Perhaps someone you feel neutral about. Maybe it's a co-worker or someone you passed by in the grocery store or at the bank. I want you to choose someone that you don't really have any particular feelings for. Go through all of the questions above and notice the differences between how the energy feels when you were doing the meditation about someone you loved versus someone you don't have any particular feelings for. Again, I want you to notice the subtle shifts of energies when you go through each question, and, also, notice how they might feel different.

I think by now, you know where this is going: After a couple times of trying this exercise, I want you to do this meditation sitting with someone that you don't like.

Maybe it's a co-worker that you don't get along with. Maybe it's your boss. Maybe it's someone who's wronged you in some large way or some small way. Maybe it's just someone who didn't let you merge in traffic or someone who took the last donut in the break room. Maybe it's someone that has different political views or values than you. Maybe it's an ex-husband or ex-wife. I want you to challenge yourself and pick somebody that has rubbed you the wrong way. Try the meditation again and go through the same questions.

Can you sit with them?

Do you notice the resistance and the openness?

Invite Wu Wei.

Does this change the meditation for you?

I know this is difficult, and it might take a few weeks to get through even just one time, and that's okay. Take your time. There is no rush.

When you feel ready, I want you to do the meditation again, but this time with yourself. I want you to go through all the same questions as you sit with yourself. This could be a younger version of yourself, or it could be you now.

Can you feel your wounds?

Can you just sit with them? Can you become them?

What do you need to tell yourself to let yourself know that you feel your own pain?

Notice the differences in energy. Notice the differences in resistance and openness between how you felt when you did this meditation with someone you didn't like versus when you did it with yourself.

Here is the key

When you practice this meditation over time, I want you to alternate between people you love, people you don't have any feelings toward, people you don't like, and yourself. I want you to become very familiar with the subtle differences in these energies and how you feel based upon who you're sitting across from.

Over time, you will be able to shift these energies ever so slightly within yourself by pulling in the energy that is needed. For example, if you're around someone you don't like, you will be able to shift and respond to the energy as if it's someone you do like. You will be able to feel the subtle differences and respond to them accordingly. When you begin to name these differences and know these different energies, that's when you can begin to shift them. As you may imagine, this became a very helpful tool for me in prison. It took me many months and hundreds of hours of practice to master, but it helped me learn about compassion, not just for those around me in prison but also for myself.

This meditation is just a small tool to help us become one with our enemy. This meditation can help you learn how to hold compassion in the body for people who think, believe, and look different from you, or even for people that may want to cause you harm. Seeing someone else as your very self begins the transformation process, which allows you to see just how connected we all are.

My friends,

I have intentionally decided to end the **Meditations** section here so you can be present to the rest of the book, which I think is important. This is where I leave you. It has been an honor and a joy spending this time, and I want to thank you for being with me in my meditations. I sincerely hope you have found them helpful. I thank you for taking the time to be present with me, and I hope you enjoy the rest of my story.

In gratitude,
R.G. Shore

R.G. Shore

PART III

Chapter Twelve

Anahata

Winter storms affect men in prison the same way they affect people on the outside. The darkness and ice bring a different kind of loneliness than the one we are already experiencing. Storms on the coast remind me of how powerless I am, as if I needed reminding. At night, the lightning surges and crackles through the dark, blanketed sky. The rain, like an angry stepfather, rages powerfully and comes at us from all directions. We can hear tree branches snapping and breaking in the distance. The ice freezes the wood in the trees. The wood expands and then explodes like a firework. The wind howls and whistles against the windows, knocking books from shelves and photos from bulletin boards. All this metal here acts as a natural conductor for the lightning. During storms, I feel so little — much littler than I already am.

By morning everything is down. The power is out, and the compound is dark and cold. The prison has a backup generator, but it's mainly used for security. Even that sometimes goes out. The powerlines are tangled in distant tree branches that hover thirty feet over the battered ground. The ice beats down on everything. This place is littered with fallen branches, splintered wood, snow, and ice, which, given this concreted jungle, makes it near impossible to walk anywhere. We are trapped in with the darkness, drenched in our denim.

When the power goes out, we go on lockdown: we

can't leave our bunks. There's nowhere to go. We can't even go to chow. They bring food to us in brown paper bags: Boloney sandwiches on moth-eaten white bread, small hard red apples — the kind that take your teeth (if you have any left) — a bag of chips, and a plastic-tasting cookie.

Thankfully, I have food in a storage box under my bed from commissary (prison's version of an overpriced 7-Eleven, with fewer selections and a lot more items that have long expired.) Unfortunately, without power, there is no microwave, which means no spreading. Without power, we have limited hot water — so no hot soups, coffee, or hot showers. The electronics are clearly shot, and we're told to unplug our TVs. If the power comes back on, it could surge the outlets and fry our idiot boxes.

During power outages, there is about as much to do as there is sitting in an empty storage unit; men get angry when they have nothing to do. With the electricity out, stress boxes don't work either, so there's no one to call and complain to. When you have zero communication with the outside world, it creates a panic within you. There's a weariness to having zero control. You think we'd be used to it by now, but I'm not sure anyone ever gets used to it.

There's a sinking feeling that happens when you realize you have no way of letting your friends and family know you're okay. The sinking feeling gets even heavier when you realize you have no way of knowing if they are okay either. The disconnection can be paralyzing. The not-knowing creates a fear, which stays in the body and stimulates the amygdala in the brain. There's little I can do to prevent the impending panic of these men. All I can do is wait for it to blow, like steam from a whistling kettle. Somehow during storms, everything becomes more racist, and, like on the outside, the blame seems to always fall on the minorities.

I sit on my bunk quietly. The wool, gray, blankets are cold and stiff against my body. The dorm is still dark. Most of the men pace back and forth, up and down the aisles of the bunks, like caged elephants. I watch one man get up from his bunk, go to the day room, sit down for thirty seconds in a plastic chair, get up again, go back to his bunk, and repeat the process all over again.

There is no stillness here. People can't stand to be with themselves. None of these men can handle it, but most men on the outside can't handle it either. Stillness is like standing in ice water. I once heard someone say that most of the world's problems were started by men who couldn't sit still in a room together. I think there's some real truth to that.

I watch another inmate get up from his bunk and walk toward the phonebooths in the back. He picks up the phone and tries to push the buttons. He clicks the hook switch up and down violently with his fingers, over and over.

"Power's out, fucking idiot!" I hear another man yell.

"Shut the fuck up," he yells back.

The dorm is wrapped in cold; inmates are either rolled up in their blankets with their beanies over their eyes or walking around aimlessly, rubbing their hands together. It seems to summarize the underlying patterns in most of the men — these men cannot stand being with themselves.

Darkness is a funny thing; it brings out the truth. As I sit here, I wonder how many of these men have ever reflected on their lives, on themselves, or on the truth of who they are beneath their skin. For the most part, we aren't afforded the luxury of safe reflection in here. Consciousness and transformation aren't as accessible to people trying to survive at a fundamental level. It's difficult thinking about how to heal when you're constantly hyper-focused on who's behind you and how you can stay safe.

When the darkness comes and we have no way of busying ourselves from its deeper truths, that's when the death creeps in — and it creeps in unexpectedly. The pain and grief can be too much to bear, but when we sit with ourselves, even for a moment, there is a glimpse of light in the shadows — that is the work. You can't die without dying. The problem is that most people want to skip right to the resurrection. Dying in here reminds us of our fragility, and powerful men don't want to be reminded of that.

A few months ago, an inmate in here died from a heart attack. I'm not sure how long the man had been down, but he had been in prison quite some time. When it happened, there was a lot of chatter. The news of his death travelled quickly through the prison, and like church wives, the gossip quickly got out of hand. In a matter of minutes, it went from, "Ol' man had a heart attack," to "A guard did it. I watched him slip some shit in his food."

But that night, when the chattering stopped, it got real quiet. For the first time ever, I experienced a solitude and a quiet I had never experienced here in prison. In general, men tend to shed their testosterone at night. On that night, I knew all the men were thinking the same thing: I don't want to die in prison.

Men in here go to sleep scared by the idea of death, but by morning, they welcome it in all the wrong ways. In here, things are primal, and we're just trying to survive physically. But when given the space, our minds can wander, and a wandering mind has the power to do terrible things to us. This is the endless death, much worse than our physical one.

There are little deaths and larger deaths in life. The little deaths creep up on us unexpectedly, shattering our expectations of what might seemingly be called a good day on the outside: spilling coffee on our work clothes, being stuck at a red light, sleeping through the alarm, running out of hot water, listening to the neighbor's dog bark endlessly while trying to work from home. The little deaths are the chainsaws breaking through the silence of our meditation.

Spirituality teaches us to allow the little deaths, even welcome them if we can. Breathwork is the path that leads to welcoming what we can't control. In prison, however, all we have are our little deaths. In here, every moment is a little death, requiring us to let go of what we never had in the first place.

The larger deaths are more unexpected, I think. They create the container that can lead to transformation, if we're willing to go there, but this kind of death only comes when we're ready for it. The larger death takes on many forms, but it comes to us in a way that will certainly challenge us uniquely and on an individual level: divorcing a partner after thirty years of marriage, losing a child, becoming an addict, losing a home to foreclosure, getting fired from a company after twenty years, getting in a car accident and becoming paralyzed from the waist down, losing a parent, or a spouse... going to prison. The larger death involves losing the one thing you thought would make you great. Only through sitting with it are we able to see that the whole thing was a hoax anyway.

With the power out now, there's nothing I can do but sit with the darkness. I try to welcome it the best I can. I pull my beanie over my eyes and sit cross-legged on my bunk. My spine is straight, and my hands are relaxed. I do my best to try to locate where I feel the sadness of the dark. There is a grief in me, but it's hard to figure out where I hold it in my body. My intuition says it's probably held in my lower back. As I focus on my back, it starts to get tight and hot, like a trampoline in the sun.

I can hear my neighbor coughing just feet away from me. His coughs come violently and often. I open my eyes, pull up my beanie, and look over.

"You good?" I ask.

He turns and looks at me.

"Don't fucking talk to me, fucking sand nigger," he replies, coughing up his lungs.

"Fair enough," I say to myself.

I grab my radio and headphones from my bookshelf, put my headphones over my ears, and click the radio on. I let the white noise drown out my neighbor's racist coughs. There is a never-ending energy of death in this place, and my body craves a different kind of force. The dorm feels heavy, and my body feels like it's weighted down by a heavy blanket. The power outage only increases the fear my body feels. The anger and hate, the racism and aggression sometimes feel too much. My radio helps to calm the death feeling. The white noise softens my rage.

I can feel myself boiling inside me. Though externally quiet, inside I'm bursting — I'm screaming underwater. I want to rage. I want to grow two feet taller. I want to grow muscles the size of tree trunks and destroy this place. I want to beat everyone with my arms. I want to strangle and dismantle these stupid, racist, pieces of shit. This is the thought I have, but I take a deep breath in and let that thought pass. It starts to come back, and I take another deep breath and have to let that thought pass too. This is the dying process.

I turn toward the window and look out at the icy trees in the distance. The world blanketed in ice makes everything white. The light outside illuminates the darkness of the dorm like a cell phone in a movie theater. I watch the icicles dangle from the trees' needles and branches. It reminds me of Christmas, but Christmas has long passed. There's a slight breeze, which causes the branches to sway and some of the icicles to fall from the needles. They make shattering sounds as they hit the ground below.

The rattling of the wind against the window and the shattering of ice begin to create a slow rhythm within me. Like ancient drums, the sounds lead me beneath my skin and into a deeper vibration. The cold of the dorm brings me into my body quicker. My skin feels restricted and tight. I do my best to just try to feel it.

I remember reading about monks in the Himalayas who could meditate so deeply that they could feel the space between their lip and their nose. I ignored my body for so long sometimes I'm not sure where to start. So, I focus on my fingers and move up the arm, scanning my body. I focus on my breath and its fire. I welcome it in and allow it to pass through me. I try to let it stay. I try to let it teach me.

When I inhale, I can feel my breath pushing against my diaphragm, like a river pushing up against a dam. It's all I have. As I inhale, I say the word "rise" quietly to myself. I imagine all the things that rise. I imagine a gentle sun and the air in the coolness of the morning. I imagine myself leaving this place. There is a warmth in the rising. I imagine all the goodness of life, even now:

Hot coffee. Going on dates in college. Night drives. Playing piano and singing. Cooking scrambled eggs and sausage. Camping on the Oregon Beach. Solo road trips in my '94 Honda Civic. Going to Europe with my high school friends. Making homemade pizza. Becoming Catholic. Discovering Buddhism and Taoism. Indoor soccer. Learning to surf. Wim Hof showers in the winter. Going to college football games. Smoking pot and writing music. Writing college term papers while drinking wine. Making bonfires on the beach and playing guitar. The smell of red peppers in a pan. *Rising.*

I slowly feel a natural humming taking place deep within me. I try to listen to the sounds that my body makes. I start to see the same lights on the back of my eyelids. As I focus on the different parts of my body, the lights change colors. My lower back puts off a reddish hue; my heart, green; my stomach, yellow. I raise my awareness and attention to the top of my head, purple. This is no coincidence. I know these colors; these are my chakras.

Chakras are wheels in the body where the energy is stored. Our body holds and carries energy everywhere. Sometimes trauma and pain in our life causes blockages in these chakras, and then the energy gets trapped.

I've learned to sit with my body in a way that opens

and frees these trapped energies. When you sit with the occluded parts of your body, you can begin to listen to the trauma kept within them. This is what I'm doing. I'm naming the trauma and locating where it is. Naming it helps me to recognize it. In giving it a name, I'm able to release it. (I imagine this is what Jesus meant when he asked the demon its name. He was releasing someone's trauma just by naming it.)

The hurt comes in cycles though. I'm learning to see the patterns within me. I'm learning to see that the patterns are cyclical, pointing to an even deeper wound. I breathe in and notice the energy, always held in my lower back, sometimes crushing into my sides and stomach just below my ribs. I just try to sit and notice it.

I hold the inhale as long as I can. I let the stillness come in and wash over me like a wave on the ocean. In this moment, there is a joy. I wish I could describe it, but then it would ruin the whole thing. All the parts of my body soften. All the tension slowly melts. I am not in those moments; I am in this moment. But I understand that each of those moments are still very much a part of this one. This is presence. In this inhale, in this dark, cold dorm, I am present to the *isness*. I am Wu Wei.

I hold the air in, maybe for minutes. The light grows brighter within me. It feels like I am walking out of a cave that I have been in for years. I can feel my hands raising up to my eyebrows, like I'm shielding the light from the sun.

Suddenly, without warning, I'm somewhere else — a familiar cafeteria. I see my younger self again. He's sitting at a table by himself with his hood up. He's wearing a dark green

Vans sweatshirt with white lettering, black jeans, and a pair of Nikes. It feels like a normal September morning, but it's not.

I walk over to my younger self who seems to recognize me now.

"Can I sit?" I ask.

"Sure," he says. "Your funeral."

"You good?" I ask him.

He doesn't respond.

After a few moments, a student walks by and glares at my younger self. I see my younger self look up at him.

"What?" he asks the kid.

The kid doesn't respond but just walks off.

A few minutes later, another kid walks by the table.

"My dad says this is your fault," he says to the thirteen-year-old me.

Up in the prison, I can feel my body twitch and my legs spasm. I know this moment. My meditation has led me into a buried memory, only it's more than a memory; I'm reliving it for the first time. It's Wednesday, September 12, 2001, the day after the attack on the Twin Towers. Everything is fresh; everyone is reactive. I'm just a thirteen-year-old kid, but it doesn't matter. I'm an easy target.

Two days ago, I was worried about acne and girls and having the right pair of Nikes. I'm only thirteen — these are the things that I care about. I'm a Brown kid in a really racist town, just trying to fit in. I've always been different —I know this — but after 9/11, I was reminded of just how different I was.

I am not sure I realized it then as much as it just gradually crept up on me: the amount of looks and "go back to your country" comments I got over the subsequent years. My high school experience was filled with the invasion of Iraq. I distinctly remember the Statue of Saddam falling during Operation Iraqi Freedom. I remember watching it in the high school commons, and I remember people glancing over at me as they watched it too. I remember the countless "America" grunts I got as I walked through the halls.

My high school years were peppered with a language of fear: weapons of mass destruction, the Global War on Terror, Muslims, terrorists. It was fear that convinced America to go to war, and it was that same fear that convinced America that anyone who looked like me must be a terrorist.

I remember going on vacation to Hawaii just a couple years after the attack on the towers. I went with my brother, my dad, and my dad's best friend (both White, while my brother and I are not). I remember being in the airport waiting for our flight when two men came up to us dressed in security suits. They said they were doing random bag and security checks, and we had been randomly selected. We all got up to follow, but they stopped my dad and his friend.

"No, just them."

My brother and I were fifteen and sixteen at the time. I could barely grow facial hair and didn't even have a driver's license, but it didn't matter. We were Brown in a White world driven by fear. This was our reality; this has always been our reality.

I was born in India but adopted by a White family.

I was born in one of the most populated cities in the world, Calcutta, a city with nearly fifteen million people in it. The entire state of Oregon is about four million.) Calcutta is one of the most spiritual and colorful places in the entire world. It is also one of the poorest. It's a place I have never known, and yet, a place I feel so connected to. India is my birthplace, but I have no memory of it.

Despite the way I look, this country is all I've ever known. I was adopted by White parents into a White family. I used to joke that I was like an Oreo: Brown on the outside but very White on the inside. I was loved by my parents (I still am) but loved in a way that reflects the culture they come from. My Brownness is something they've never understood — how could they?

Oregon is one of the only places in the U.S. where you can wake up on the beach and be mountain climbing by the end of the day. But while it is known for its liberal PNW vibes, backpacking, hiking, and love for Subarus, it also carries a very racist past that often bleeds into the present.

Oregon began as Whites-only state, which still today, makes up over eighty percent of the state's population. (Black people make up less than two percent of Oregon's population.) It wasn't until 2002 that Oregon finally amended its state constitution to remove racial references like "negroes" and "mulattos" from it. (Though it passed, thirty percent of the voters still voted "no" on removing the language from the state's constitution. I read a New York Times article not too long ago that suggested Portland is the Whitest city in the U.S. today.)

In my high school, I was surrounded by a lot of good ol' White country boys who drove around in oversized trucks, waving their confederate flags while revving their engines loud enough to match their White anger. It was the kind of anger that caused kids to do things like buy tacos to throw at "the Mexicans" or to tell people like me to go back to my own country.

I wasn't White, but I wasn't really Indian either, which made things worse. I was constantly in no man's land — caught between two worlds, neither here nor there. I didn't have the Indian culture. I couldn't speak Hindi. I didn't know the Vedic traditions. When people asked me about Krishna, I just smiled. When I got to college, the assumptions didn't go away. I remember going to a church event and meeting a pastor for the first time.

When he shook my hand, he said, "You speak really good English."

"You speak really good English too," I replied with humor, my greatest defense mechanism.

"Are your parents Hindi?" he asked.

"No — they're Catholic."

"Oh... sorry. So, you go to the University of Oregon?" he asked, changing the subject.

"Yep," I replied.

"Math major?" he asked again.

"Nope."

"Oh, IT?"

Though seemingly innocuous, even my colloquial experiences were inherently racist.

As I sit here in my meditation, at this table in this cafeteria with my thirteen-year-old self, I realize a subtle truth: in some way, it has always felt like that Wednesday after the attack on the towers.

I turn back to my younger self. I can see he doesn't know how to process what's happening to him. I'm not sure I know how to process what's happening to me now.

"Sorry," I tell him.

"It doesn't matter," he responds.

"Yes, it does," I reply, but I know I can't take away the hurt that he'll experience.

How do I let go of trying to protect the parts of me I know I can't protect? How do I let go of the hurt inside? I can see it begin to take place right before me — the dying process. It's a letting go of who we never were but always wanted to be. It's a fire that burns away all the possibilities that were never actually possible.

He looks at me, and, for the first time, I think he knows who I am. It's a weird feeling. I can feel my lower back begin to ache and pulse from my prison bunk.

"You know me?" he asks, but with a certainty.

"Yes," I reply.

"Does it get better?" he asks.

"There are good days and bad days," I respond gently.

He doesn't say anything, but I know what he's thinking, because I finally know what I'm thinking. Through my meditations, I am learning to be gentle with the younger parts of myself because they, too, are longing to be seen. In this moment, I begin to piece it together.

I always knew I looked different, but I think I compartmentalized just how different I felt. When you look different, you feel less a part of people. You feel less connected. I wanted so badly to fit in; I wanted so badly to feel good enough. I felt like I had to work twice as hard just to be like everybody else. I got really good at things and became talented because that was how I knew I could gain people's approval.

When you're a Brown kid in a White place, you learn to adapt. You get good at just surviving. I was smart and witty and talented — this helped. The problem was, while I got good at being talented, I was never allowed the luxury of just being. I grew up in a place that didn't celebrate people's differences, so I didn't learn to celebrate my own. I had to be White, but I was never White enough to keep up. No matter how talented, smart, or capable I was, at the end of the day, I was still Brown.

"Don't worry," I say to him. "I got you."

"I believe you," he says.

As I look at my younger self in this meditation, I realize he is still very much a part of my present self, held somewhere in my lower back. The trauma and hurt is kept there, blocked in with some energy that hasn't been released yet. My whole life I've felt different, and in the end, the place I get sent for punishment is a place that reminds me just how different I am — day in, day out, in the worst possible ways.

I wonder if it's a joke. It's too tragicomic not to be. I wonder if there is some divine being up there pulling strings, smoking a cigar, and turning to his other divine buddies, saying, "Watch this." For a moment, I get angry, but then my younger self says something to me that changes everything.

"Thanks for helping me."

I pause. The realization of what he's said hits me fast,

like an epiphany.

I realize in this moment that I am helping him, like actually helping him. It's more than just a release of trauma that's been held captive by some memory of my younger self. In some real, deep way, I am helping my younger self in his time too.

What power do we have to change what was? I don't know. Perhaps, there is a profound truth to time being relative. I've never understood quantum physics. I don't even understand how a microwave works, let alone quantum or time, but after this breakthrough with my younger self, I feel like I do know myself, all parts of me. And when my younger self tells me that I am helping him, I believe him.

Do we have the power to help the younger versions of ourselves? Is there, in fact, a power to send energy and love to those parts of us in those times that came before?

I remember reading an idea in quantum physics called the observer effect, which suggests that, at the quantum level, the very act of observing something changes the thing being observed. Does the simple act of me interacting with — seeing — my younger self change him on some deeper level?

My intuition tells me that it does. Perhaps, things aren't as linear as we'd like to believe.

As I watch this version of my younger self smiling back at me, deep in this meditation, I feel calm and at ease. As absurd as this is, isn't this just prayer? Divine energy finding us where we need it, when we need it? Somehow, I know that love meets us where we are at, and that is enough.

"I'm not sure how it will go. I'm not sure what the end looks like, but I do know that the only way to heal is through," I tell him.

"What does that mean?" he asks.

"It means you have to sit with the stuff that you don't want to sit with. You have to be okay with the sad things that you don't want to feel."

"I don't know what I don't want to sit with," my younger self responds.

"That's okay. You will. Trust your body. It will lead you in the end."

"Okay," he says.

"Can you do me a favor?" I ask him.

"What?" he replies.

"Will you sit and meditate with me for a bit?"

"I don't know how," he responds.

"Just breathe in, and then breathe out. Breathe in and follow it, and breathe out and follow it."

For the first time ever, I sit with my young self, and we breathe together. My present self and my younger self, held together, breathing as one. In this moment, wherever this moment is, I am present to it. Alive to it. Compassionate to it.

I'm not sure how time works, but it's not linear. Spirituality isn't linear. The healing isn't linear. Because we are here together, my present self and my younger self, breathing together, learning together as one. I am beginning to see that the parts that made me different were always included, and the parts that made me feel so far from everyone else were the same parts that made me feel more connected to everything else. When you learn to see God in yourself, you begin to see God everywhere.

With my eyes closed, I exhale and say the word "fall" quietly to myself. I allow the breath to leave me. When I let go, I feel the light leaving. Just as there is a warmth in the rising, there is a coolness in the falling. I begin to feel the hurt, and I imagine all the things that fall. When I exhale, I imagine the shame and the brokenness of my life, even now:

Having Brown skin. Being Indian. Being adopted. Growing up in a racist town. Not being tall enough. Feeling ugly. Not getting as good of grades as my friends. Not feeling smart enough. Being single. Gambling. Inappropriate relationships. Unhealthy relationships. Student loan debt. Loneliness. Depression. Not feeling White enough. Failing at jobs. Not feeling like I was ever good enough for the White God I was told to believe in. Hurting people around me. Getting arrested. Going to prison. *Falling.*

When you grow up in a system that encourages punishment, people aren't taught how to hold the "both/and." People aren't taught how to feel hurt while also welcoming the reconciliation and rehabilitation. In life, there are consequences, and there should be. But I'm just not sure prison is a necessary one — ever. I don't think prison ever really heals anything. I don't think shame ever really heals anything either.

The yang energy requires us take responsibility for our actions, to sit with the hurt that we've caused others, as well as the trauma within ourselves. The yin energy is the calming and nurturing energy that reminds us everything belongs and everything is included, including the hurt. When I feel the energy of yin, it reminds me that I'm never too far from an energy of love that has always held me. But in a place like prison, yang is often the only energy one feels.

In this moment, in this meditation, the sadness and grief feel overwhelming. I feel so embarrassed. I feel so ashamed. I breathe in slowly and breathe out slowly. I let my breath guide me. I listen to my body. Then, in the quiet of this moment, in the pulsing of my grief, I hear a subtle voice within me:

Anahata.

Your heart, it is boundless.

Anahata is the name of the heart chakra. It is the chakra that connects the lower chakras and higher chakras. It is the bridge between what was and what will be. The Anahata chakra is the home to change. It holds the grief, and it also holds the possibility of letting go of that grief. It is the link between the physical and spiritual. The heart leads us to transformation. It carries us away from the shame and into the hands of what has always held us — love.

I open my eyes. I'm back in prison and on my bunk. The yin and yang of my life summed up with a single breath — inhale and exhale. Something has shifted in me. I'm not quite sure what it is, but I know I'm going to be okay. Somehow, in waking up from this meditation, I know now that the Universe is for me; the Universe is on my side.

I can feel that my failures were never really failures because they were always a part of something much larger than themselves. I now know that I was slowly being led to a place internally where I could finally include them.

I turn off my radio and wind my headphones up and place them on my shelf. I take a deep breath in and out and look out the window at the icy trees. The clouds are gray, but there is a hint of sun behind them, not yet poking through. Ice crystals still hang from the needles of the trees. I sit silently thinking about my meditation, not yet sure how to process my interaction, but something feels calmer within me now. Something feels more alive and awake. I watch as the breeze gently makes her way through the fir trees. Then, out of the corner view of my window, in the distant trees, I spot them walking into view.

A doe and her fawn tenderly walk across the grass outside the gated fence. I watch them stop underneath the trees and munch on some frozen leaves. It's surreal seeing something so spiritual take place before your very eyes — the most beautiful thing, in the ugliest place. I watch as the doe turns to her fawn and begins to lick her matted fur. She cleans her from head to tail. She is her protector. Then I watch as they gently walk back into the trees, away from the prison.

Chapter Thirteen

Out of the Jar

I had a vision once, sometime during my college years. I remember I was on my way to a concert up in Portland with my friends. I was sitting in the passenger seat with my head against the window, looking out at the passing fields. The sky was overcast, but there was an aperture in the clouds where the sun was peeking through over the shaded valley. The different colors of patchwork farms, variegated in Oregon greens, began to blend together. Suddenly, the light from the sun pierced the land and all turned to a bright light.

In that moment, I saw my body, and I saw everybody else's body begin to melt. As the light hit the car, our bodies began to melt into light and into waves. And in that vision, I saw that we were all just waves on a vast ocean — different waves, but the same water — moving into each other and out from each other, flowing as one. Sometimes the waves crashed into each other, but other times they just melted together and became one. In this vision, I realized that in the end, we are all just movement. That is all life is; we are all waves, I think. This is not a sad realization, but perhaps the most beautiful one there could be.

I've come to realize that prison is the second-hardest place to heal. The hardest place to heal is a place where people no longer think you're worthy of the healing. Over time, you begin to believe the lie, and you start to think you're no longer worthy of healing either. I have since learned that my healing is not determined by whether or not people think I deserve it.

The problem is we live in a country that encourages the wound. Our country would rather create groups of people to blame than help those people grow and heal. Our country has a young mind, and a young mind is a dualistic mind; it needs people to hate. In my experience, punishment doesn't heal the wound; it only enlarges it. Like those in prison, we are a country permeated in yang energy. Perhaps it's time that we become more receptive toward the yin within: compassion, patience, gentleness, allowing, nurturing, and intuitiveness.

Trapping men in a cage where there is no healing or mending of the hurt does not isolate the hurt; this is one of the greatest misconceptions of our country's time, a reflection of its immaturity and its poverty. We think we can isolate the hurt by putting people away who have caused it, but, like love, hurt is never an isolated thing. It flows everywhere. It is in all things and connected to all things. My hurt becomes your hurt, becomes her hurt, becomes his hurt, becomes they're hurt, — that is why it is so painful. When we create rules and laws that no longer allow people to heal, we are no longer able to heal ourselves either.

Spirituality is not an isolated thing. It is all connected to the same source underneath. Your journey is never just your journey alone. Everybody's path is unique to their own experience — and God, the Universe, love, or whatever you wish to call it, comes to each one of us uniquely and individually in its own way, in its own time; but that journey is still connected to all other journeys. In the end, your path is not separate from my path; this is the second greatest misconception of our country's time, a reflection of its spiritual immaturity and its spiritual poverty. We cannot think healing ourselves does not involve the healing of everybody else too.

Prison has taught me that my journey is also your journey; your wound is also my wound. As long as we punish certain groups of people and put them away, we only punish ourselves and put ourselves away. The hate we have for others is the hate we have for ourselves. My Brownness is also these White supremacists' Brownnesss too. Their racist wounds are also my racist wounds too. I am now not just myself. I am all incarcerated people. I am all their pain, but I am also all their healing too.

During my time in prison, I have learned to be still, like the towering evergreens in the quiet of the forest. In my stillness, I now listen to the wisdom of my body — each part. And each part of me tells a story that has longed to be told. In this jungle of a prison, no one ever stops. It all just keeps going, and everybody keeps moving, keeps hustling. But I have learned to stop and to observe the stillness that is always available within me, even here. It's the damnedest thing: to find healing inside of the wound. The Brownness that once made me different is the same Brownness that now empowers me.

In the months that have followed, I have learned to sit with myself in new ways. During meditation, I send love and energy to my younger self. I have realized that I can be the help he was looking for. I can send him the love that he needs — even now. I don't necessarily think I can change his outcome, but I can send him an energy that prepares him for what's coming. I can be his sustainer. For so long, I hid the parts of me I did not wish to face — these parts have ended up being my greatest parts.

When we, my younger self and I, meet in the dark moments of the night, through the gentle static of rain and ocean from my radio, I prepare him and let him know he is going to be okay, because I am okay now. Just as he reaches out for my help, I reach out for help from a version of my future self who I know will one day send energy and love to me now, in this moment. There is a version of me somewhere ahead of me, sustaining me, holding me, and letting me know I am going to be okay, too.

I have learned that I can do this for myself, and I can do this for others, too. The voice I hear in my meditation — maybe it's God, the Universe, or maybe it's just me from some other time, in some other place — letting me know it's got me. We are all little divine universes after all, discovering ourselves is the greatest gift we could be given. I am not certain of much, but I am certain there is a love that gently holds us and sustains us in all things.

I don't use my radio as much anymore. Sometimes I still need it, especially to get through all the snoring and all the anger that habitually surrounds me, but for the most part, it sits on my shelf beside my bunk, behind my books. I can call on the static and the quiet of the ocean within me. It still takes time, but it does come. Of course, there are good days, and there are bad days.

I wake up early. The dorm is already hot and muggy. It

feels like a swamp in here. It's a July morning, and the summer sun is beating through the window, heating up the metal on my bunk. My arm is stiff and red from light pouring in through the window. I can hear birds in the distance. It's 7 a.m., but it feels like 3 p.m. I can already smell the sweat and hot iron from the yard. I can hear the clanging of metal and the clinking chains from the inmates working out on the yard. I hear their powerful grunts in the distance.

After making some instant coffee, I put on my jeans and lace up my shoes. I make my way out of the dorm and up through the first and second gate toward the law library. I've got a relaxed day for the most part — there's just one inmate coming to see me.

I climb the stairs and make my way past the admin building and into the law library. The room is hot and stuffy. The summer dust has caked the covers of the law books. One by one, I take each book outside of the building and dust it off with my hand. I watch the dust blow out into the gentle air. The breeze takes some dust with it, while the rest falls to the ground of the parking lot. The sun beats fiery hot on the concrete and pavement. I feel beads of sweat begin to form on the back of my shoulders. I bring the books back in and set them next to the table near my computer. I remove the plastic bag from the fan, plug it in, and let the air circulate around the room for a few minutes. It still feels like it's a hundred degrees in here. I sit down at my computer to study, and then I see a nine-by-twelve envelope addressed to me.

What's this? I wonder.

I open the envelope. Inside there is a small letter of congratulations with a certificate attached. It's my paralegal certificate. I've passed the program with distinction and honors; I'm an official paralegal now. It took me a year and some change to complete, but I'm proud of my accomplishment. I've helped a lot of people in here. I've saved over a thousand months of inmate's sentences and over one million in fines and fees from civil lawsuits. I open my law journals and begin to study when I hear a knock at the door.

"It's open," I say.

In walks an inmate with a mask covering his face. He has stringy, greasy black hair, and fingernails that are long and pointed like daggers. He takes off his mask. His teeth are jagged like a vampire, and he has a cross on his arm bent like a swastika. It's my old neighbor.

He grunts right away. I can tell I'm the last person he wants help from.

He sits down in a chair six feet away from me and stares at the bookshelf. He doesn't talk.

I decide to speak first.

"How can I help?" I ask.

He grunts again. He is avoiding eye contact, but I know he needs my help. I feel bad for him. He's a thirty-something-year-old man, but he can't ask me for help. He has too much pride and too much fear. When I look at him, I just see a scared child.

"It's okay," I tell him. "It's okay to ask for help. No one will know. You can ask. I won't tell anyone I helped you."

"Fine," he finally says begrudgingly. "I think I've got the thing everybody's talking about, but they won't treat me."

"What thing?" I ask.

"The Coronavirus thing," he says. "I can't really smell or taste anything."

"Okay. I'll see what I can do," I reply, putting on a mask and rubbing my hands with hand sanitizer. I turn back to my computer and begin reviewing DOC administrative rules on medical procedures.

The prison has been shut down from the outside for several months. In March, they stopped all visits from friends and family. Somehow, COVID started spreading around the prison compound. It's a funny thing: we can't leave, we haven't gone anywhere, so how did we get it? The guards are pretty vocal about it not being a real big deal and "just another way for the government to spy on us," so they're the ones bringing it into the prison. You're worrying about the government spying on you? You work for the DOC, it's a funny irony.

The prison has been infected with COVID for a few months now. DOC picks and chooses how and when they want to comply with the statewide mandates. They don't let us have visitors anymore, which feels illegal because they don't provide money for phone calls out to friends and family members. There's no way to stay connected unless you have money coming in from the outside. They should at least give money to inmates who are indigent (who don't have enough money to make a single phone call to their wife or their kids).

I haven't seen friends or family in months since they shut down the prison from the outside world. I talk to my parents on the phone occasionally. They say everything is shut down out there too. They say everyone is cooped up and isolated. It's funny thinking about how isolated people feel out there, almost like a leveling of the playing field. It's interesting hearing about people on the outside feeling trapped in their own homes — I would give anything to be home.

They make us walk six feet apart to chow, but when we get to the chow hall, we sit and eat inches away from each other. To keep things less crowded, they only allow certain dorms on the yard at a time, but after yard, we go right back to our overcrowded, crammed dorms and sit on our bunks that are only two feet apart. It's a formality, but nothing has really changed. They won't give us tests unless we're already showing signs and symptoms. From what I've heard, if you're showing symptoms, it's already too late. There is continual coughing in the dorms. Some men sweat it out. I can hear the hacking and retching in the bathroom. Regardless of people's opinions about it, one thing's for sure: there is nothing worse than having COVID in prison.

It took us a month or so to get tests available. I did a lot of work researching and writing up request forms with proper procedural language, requesting that the DOC bring tests into the prison and make them available for us. They finally complied, but now, when they test the inmates, they send them right back to dorm to wait for the test results, which exposes the rest of us in the interim. The test results take about three days. So, even if the tests come back negative, there's no real way to tell if the inmates are negative because they've just sent them back down to the same dorm where they got exposed in the first place; it makes the whole thing moot.

For the first couple of months, they wouldn't give us facemasks. I did the research and found that it violated DOC admin rules to not follow proper health guidelines implemented by the state. They finally gave us facemasks, but the masks are made from cloth or denim from old prison jeans. I feel pretty sure wearing denim over our mouths doesn't really prevent the virus from spreading. They want to make it look like they're keeping us safe, but I'm not convinced they care. They've sent all the old men out of this prison and relocated them to the State Pen where they have faster access to healthcare, but I think they're just worried about liability because this prison doesn't even have an onsite doctor. He's on call every Friday. Sometimes, he doesn't show up.

"What are you wanting me to help with exactly?" I ask my old neighbor. "Are you looking to be tested? Are you looking to be shipped out to a different prison?"

"They won't give me a test," he responds.

"Why?"

"Dunno, they just won't."

"Did you ask Medical?" I ask.

"Yeah, they said I'm not showing any signs, but I told them I can't taste anything."

"And what did they say to that?" I ask.

"Dunno, nothing really."

It's true. In prison, if someone doesn't want to give you something, they just don't. It's as simple as that, and there's nothing you can do about it — usually.

I pull out a DOC medical request form from a file cabinet.

"Fill this form out with your name here and your info here," I say, pointing to the different lines on the document.

"Is this going to do anything?" he asks me.

"Well, you fill that part out. I'll do the research with the right OARs, cite the right sources, and, hopefully, they'll give you a COVID test."

"It's fucking stupid," my old neighbor says to me. "I can't even taste anything."

"Well, given what we have for lunch, I don't think you're missing out on anything."

For the first time, he chuckles.

"That's true," he says. "Food sucks here. So, what happens if I have COVID?"

"They'll probably ship you somewhere where they can isolate and treat you," I respond.

"They better not ship me out. I got all my shit here."

"I'm sorry, man. That's just what I've heard they've been doing," I say to him.

"Am I going to come back?"

"That I can't say," I tell him.

"How am I supposed to tell my wife if I get shipped out? She won't know where I am. It's not like I fucking have money to call her."

"I don't know," I respond. "I'm sorry. I mean, I guess you don't have to get tested if you don't want to."

"Here," he says, handing me the form. "Just do it, I guess. It's better than being sick and dying in here."

He gets up, puts his facemask back on, and walks to the door. Before leaving, he pauses and looks back at me. I can tell he wants to say something, maybe thanks? But I don't know. For a moment, I think he's going to say it, but he doesn't. He just walks out.

I finish doing the research for my old neighbor and fill out the rest of the form for him. Then I spend the rest of the morning sanitizing the office. After a few hours, I close the law library and head over to the medical building where I wait to hand in his form to a nurse.

"What's this?" the nurse asks, as I hand her the document.

"Legal request for medical care," I respond. "Inmate might have COVID, needs a test."

"Don't they all," she says sarcastically.

I smile back, but don't say anything.

"Speaking of COVID. You're scheduled to come up later this afternoon," the nurse says to me. "We need to give you a test to make sure you're negative. Final checkups."

"I'll be there," I respond.

"You excited?" she asks. "You get out tomorrow, right?"

"Yep, just a wake up," I say to her. "Today's my last full day in prison."

The next morning, I wake up without an alarm. I'm too anxious to sleep. I don't know how I feel. I'm excited and nervous and scared all at the same time. It feels surreal. I've been here for almost one thousand days. I don't really know how to respond. I try to calm my body and listen to it, but it's moving around too much. Anxiety is bouncing around inside me like a pinball in a pinball machine.

I pull the sheets off my bunk and wad them up into a ball. The guard walks over with a clipboard and tells me he needs to mark some things off first.

"What for?" I ask.

"Just making sure you don't steal anything,"

"Yeah," I joke. "I'm really going to want to take these sheets with me. A little memento for the grandkids someday."

He laughs.

I continue to pack my things. I throw all my old letters and things into garbage bags, along with pens, art pads, photos, old papers, journals, and notebooks from my paralegal studies. I twist the garbage sacks up and tie a knot at the top. I put my shoes in a different bag, unscrew my TV from the bed post, box it up, and stack it next to my shoes. I lean over and empty the bookshelf of all my books. The only thing left on my shelf is my radio.

I pick it up and hold it in my hand for a few moments. It feels so light. I unravel the cords and slide my headphones over my ears.

One last time, I think to myself.

I turn the radio on and turn up the volume. I listen to the static entering my ear drums; it is as cool and as welcoming as ever. I can feel the gentle ocean come wafting in, but this time, I don't close my eyes. I don't try to meditate. This time, I just sit and listen to the white noise. It's enough.

By 8:30 a.m., all my things are in garbage bags. My parents will be here at 10 a.m.

I put the bags with all my belongings on my bunk and stack my shoes and boots next to them. Then I take my extra jeans and sweatshirt up to the guard to turn them in.

"Throw it in with the laundry."

I do as he says. I walk over to the laundry bin and throw my jeans in. I'm never going to wear blue jeans again, I tell myself.

I've still got some time to kill. I walk outside to the yard and decide to do one last lap around the track. The yard is hot and sweaty and busy. It feels surreal being out in the yard for the last time. It feels good. I look around at all the inmates, some playing cards, others basketball, many lifting weights. For them, it's just another day crammed between a thousand other days.

I make my way down to the track. It's hot and dusty, but I don't care. I walk clockwise around the track, kicking up dirt and rocks with my shoes. I focus on each crunch of gravel beneath my feet. The yard smells of body odor and hot metal, saliva and racism, but I drown it out with my breath. I finish a lap and decide to do another one, then another, and another. Without realizing it, I do twenty. Then, just like that, I hear my name being called on the intercom.

It's time for me to go home.

I go back inside the dorm and grab all the things off my bunk, and with my hands full of garbage bags, I head out of the dorm for the last time. I walk up the stairs to the first gate. It buzzes me through; I don't look back. After a few minutes, I get to the top of the second set of stairs where the Lieutenant is waiting for me.

"Well, you survived," he says to me.

"Just barely," I reply, with sweat starting to form around my brow.

"Take care of yourself," he says.

"I will," I say back to him.

He shakes my hand firmly and walks out of sight.

After a few moments, a second guard approaches me with a paper sack.

"Here," he says, shoving the sack in my already full hands. I open the bag and see a pair of clothes my parents have sent me: a clean, wool, black Patagonia fleece, a white T-shirt, and black Nike sweatpants. No denim.

The guard takes me around the corner next to the Hole and opens up a door.

"You can change in here," he says to me. "When you've finished changing, just bring your prison clothes out with you, and we'll throw them in laundry."

"Can I burn them?" I joke.

He doesn't respond.

He shuts the door, and I begin to change. It feels so different putting on a pair of pants that aren't blue jeans. It feels so odd putting on my old clothes, like I'm stepping into another time that doesn't belong to me. They don't fit great. The shirt is tight because I've gained muscle from working out for nearly three years, but I'm lean enough to make it work. I'm not sure if I can capture it, but even the feeling of having different clothes on my back makes me feel freer.

After getting dressed, I open the door and hand the guard my old prison clothes.

"Your parents are waiting at the outer gate. I'll drive you," he says.

"Okay," I respond. I put the garbage bags filled with my belongings in the back of the car and hop in the front seat. It feels weird; I haven't been in a car in a long time. Driving 30 MPH feels like 120.

"You got a job lined up?" he asks me as we pull out of the parking lot and head down toward the main gate.

"I think so," I respond. "Some family friends own a garden nursery. They need someone to water the plants for the summer."

"Sounds like a good gig," he says.

"Yeah, I think so," I respond.

After a few minutes of driving, we get to the front gates of the prison where my parents are waiting for me. I step out of the car and hug them. Everything feels slow and surreal. I don't quite have feeling in my body, but that's okay; I just want to get out of here.

"Don't come back," the CO says.

"I won't," I respond.

My dad takes my things and puts them in the back of the car. I get in the front seat and close the door. I take a deep breath in. I want to try and be present to my body for this moment. I want to remember it; I want to be fully alive in it.

My dad gets in the driver's seat and starts the car. Then, we drive off, out of sight, through the trees, and away from the prison. I can hear the gates close behind us, but I don't look back.

The hard thing about getting out of prison isn't just the world you're getting out to (a world now doused in division), but also the perspective that world has on life itself. On the outside, Tuesdays feel like Saturdays; I feel more grounded and connected to the underlying patterns all around me. All my senses are heightened in an afterglow of gratitude: I can't stop staring at all the food in the grocery stores, all the *real* cheese. I can drive into town and get a coffee when I want, or a slice of pizza. I can go to the bathroom and close the door. I can light all my jeans on fire and wear sweatpants and stay out past 9 p.m. if I want to. I can go to bed with all the lights off.

Of course, there is still a lot of trauma held in my body. Some of it might be there for the rest of my life. I don't like people standing behind me, sneaking up on me, or being too loud. I don't like crowds, and I still wake up at night just to make sure no one is standing by my bed. Yes, there is real hurt and very little help available to people like me, but getting out of prison is a rebirth, unimaginable to anyone who hasn't gotten out of prison before. For everybody else, a Tuesday is still just a Tuesday, which can make people on the outside sometimes feel just as isolated.

Two days later, I'm at my new job in a nursery, watering the plants. The July summer air is hot, but there's a slight breeze. I can hear bees buzzing around the garden, pollinating the flowers. As I wrap up a set of hoses, a hummingbird flutters past me. For a moment, it stops right in front me, hovering in midair, and I swear it looks at me. It feels odd to be surrounded by animals and creatures again. It feels dreamlike, being a part of the earth, no longer separate from her. My body feels closer and more connected here. I don't feel like I have to try as hard to be present where I am.

The smell of the garden is wonderful. It's the furthest thing from the smell of plastic, fake cheese, and concrete. The grass feels soft beneath my feet. The colors of the flowers are bright and warm and full of life. The air smells warm and like honey suckle. The garden is life-giving and full and the opposite of where I've been. Sometimes, the sadness creeps in a bit, but for the most part, I'm happy.

I take my time with each plant. I feel the leaves with my hands. I smell them. I feel their textures. It is so green here. The oxygen feels fuller and fresher. Occasionally, I find myself staring off into the garden, not realizing I've been standing in the same place, watering the same plant (probably longer than I should). The earth feels so much closer, and I feel so much more connected to her than ever before. Sometimes I whisper "thank you" to her. I'm not sure what I'm thanking her for, but I just am.

After a few hours, I head over to the orchard to water the pear and apple trees.

I drag the hose along the ground, listening to it slither as it makes its way through the tall grass. As I stop to water each tree, I spend time with them. I touch the bark and feel their leaves — no longer a fence between us. I'm allowed to eat the fruit, so I pick a pear from one of the trees and take a bite. I savor its taste. The pear is crisp and life-giving. I look out at the orchard and at the dozens of trees before me. A few moments later, my boss comes strolling into the orchard with a potted flower in his hand.

"Have you tried the Airlie Red apples?" he asks me.

"No," I respond.

"They're the best."

"What flower is that?" I ask, pointing to the pot in his hand.

"It's an Alstroemeria. Casablanca Peruvian Lily."

I look at the flower. It's a beautiful white flower with a yellowish tint and maroon dots peppered along the petals.

"Beautiful," I respond.

"I'm going to go plant it. Want to join?" he asks.

"I'm going to finish up watering here," I respond. "Thanks though."

"No problem! Douse me. I need some hydration for the long journey," my boss jokes with a smile. I point the hose upward into the sky and place my thumb on the end of the nozzle. The water sprays high up into the air and comes splashing down on him like a fountain. He gives a nervous yelp and shakes the water off like a wet dog.

"Ahhh, much better," he says to me. "You want a go?"

"Yeah," I respond. I hand him the hose, and he sprays me. The cold water cools the heat off my back, and I find myself shivering under the hot sun.

"Better?" he asks. I nod my head. "Make sure to drink lots of water. Don't give it all to the trees."

"I won't," I reply.

My boss smiles and walks out of the orchard, carrying the Alstroemeria in his hand.

"Oh, hey, by the way…" he calls back at me from a distance.

"Yeah?" I ask.

"It can get tedious watering for eight hours at a time. You're welcome to listen to a podcast or something. Feel free to bring your headphones next time if you like."

I look around at the surrounding earth and at the trees in the orchard. I can smell the honey suckle and the warm air drifting in from the distant gardens. I can hear the buzzing bees flying from petal to petal, gathering pollen on their tiny legs. There is a slight breeze that cools the hot sun on the back of my neck. I look back at my boss from across the orchard.

"Thanks," I respond. "But I think I'm good."

Epilogue

I started seeing a therapist after getting out of prison to help process my grief and trauma. (I am still learning to process it all; I'm not sure it'll ever end.) I am starting to understand that God, or Universe, or Divine Energy doesn't come to me in my pain but comes to me as my pain. Can I hold that? Can I contain it? Somehow, this tremendous form of energy, made both of love and trauma, holds all the parts of me together as one, and I am starting to learn to hold the two together within me.

A year after getting out, I decided it was time to move out of my parents' home. It was scary starting over, and I wasn't quite sure how to do it. Finding a place to rent is impossible. Nobody wants to rent to felons; no wonder there are so many on the streets. I spent months trying to apply without anyone giving me a chance. A lot of landlords and property management companies ask for three years of previous rental history. I can't really put "prison" as my previous place of residency; it's kind of a red flag. Being a felon is an automatic "no" in the renting world. I made many calls to plead my case, but it didn't matter. The reality is that most people say they support people getting out of prison and getting a second chance, but when they're given the opportunity to help, they don't.

I have a master's degree, a bachelor's degree, a completion of a paralegal program, as well as a couple years of experience as a paralegal, but it doesn't matter: I couldn't find a job anywhere. I was offered a job on the spot by several prestigious law firms. On more than one occasion, the committee stopped the interview, left the room, briefed for a few minutes, came back into the room, and told me they would love to hire me. On every occasion, the offer was rescinded when they found out I had been in prison.

After several months of looking for housing, I was finally able to convince a landlord to meet with me. The place was a little one-hundred-year-old, six-hundred-square-foot farmhouse on some country road ten miles outside the city, just fifteen minutes from the garden where I watered.

When I drove up the gravel road and into the driveway, I saw a rickety old farmhouse with a porch and swing and decaying shutters from the early 1900s. It was perfect. The kitchen and living area were one combined room downstairs with one bathroom and a loft for my bed. It was summer and was boiling, but the landlord convinced me it got cool in the fall. In the front yard was a large patch of grass, and the backyard was long enough to kick a soccer ball around. I could hear chickens from a nearby yard and a buffalo from a neighbor down the way. I told her about my record. She didn't seem to care. She was in need of someone to pay her rent. She asked me if I paid rent on time, and I said, "Yes." Then she asked me if I was a Christian, I lied, and said, "Yes." (I really needed somewhere to live.)

On the day I moved in, it was over a hundred degrees outside and hotter inside. My dad and my best friend helped me move.

"Never again," my best friend told me on multiple occasions. "I love you, man, but never again. It's too damn hot."

The landlord watched, a little too closely, and aggressively insisted on where I should put my couch, but after an hour of sweating, lifting, and moving, I had finally moved into my new place. I thanked my dad. My best friend who joked that I owed him fifty bucks for helping, and they drove off.

That same evening, on the first night in my new place, I stood outside in the front yard with my feet barefoot in the grass, and I meditated. The sun was finally coming down, and it was a perfect seventy-some-odd degrees outside. The sun peered through the tall, ancient oak trees, with a slight breeze. I was breathing deep and listening to my inhales and exhales when a car drove up the dusty driveway. I watched the blue Honda Civic come to a halt and saw a pretty woman with silver hair get out of the driver's seat.

"Hi," I said from a distance.

"Hi," she said back.

To my surprise, she came over to me, and we started talking. I found out she had just moved out of the place I had moved into. She was coming back on her last night to grab the rest of her things and say goodbye to the landlord. After talking, I learned she was a paralegal too. She asked about my bare feet, and I told her I had been meditating. She told me that she enjoyed meditating too and that it was her dream to become a yoga teacher and help people discover spirituality through movement. Our twenty-minute chat quickly turned into a four-hour-long conversation.

A year and a half later, we got married.

I became a spiritual counselor through the Urban Spirituality Center in Portland, Oregon. My wife is now working on completing her five-hundred-hour yoga program so she can help teach people to move and heal through their bodies. We started a nonprofit center where we help people engage in spiritual embodiment. Our goal has always been to help people heal, especially those who can't find healing anywhere else. I do believe the trauma within my skin, and the trauma from my incarceration, informs me in new ways.

Through that trauma, my hope is to help other people learn to sit with their own. I provide Reiki and spiritual counseling, and I teach people to listen to their bodies in ways they haven't before. I have no idea what life will look like, and that's okay. I take it one day at a time. My wife and I both send energy and love back to myself in prison. We let him know he's going to be okay.

I still meditate every day, sometimes in silence, sometimes in the rain, sometimes by the ocean — now without my headphones.

ACKNOWLEDGEMENTS

I am forever grateful for the people who have been gracious enough to see past my wounds and my shame. I am grateful for the people who continuously show up and accept all the parts of me. Jess, thank you, for your endless acceptance. Jeremy, for your gentle insight. Don, and Bill. Thank you Tom M., Mark, Phil and Jim. Mitch, Mason, and Alex. Thank you to my parents, to Sandy and Garry, and Kellie. Most importantly, I am grateful to all the parts of myself, past, present, and future.

The Divine has a wonderful way of showing up in so many different faces and people. I would be amiss if I didn't mention my gratitude toward the Universe, her little earth, and all the wonderful creatures that meet me where I am. And of course, the constellations, trees, mountains, rivers, oceans and animals, thank you.

SOURCES

I feel it is imperative to acknowledge my great teachers.
Thank you for your wisdom.

Ram Dass, Thomas Merton, Richard Rohr, Mirabai Starr,
Thich Nhat Hanh, Wim Hof, Alan Watts.

Please consider these great works of wisdom and insight for
your own spiritual journey:

Ram Dass: Experiments in Truth (Audiobook)
Thomas Merton: New Seeds of Contemplation
Richard Rohr: Falling Upward & Universal Christ
Alan Watts: The Way of Zen
Mirabai Starr: Wild Mercy
Thich Nhat Hanh: Living Buddha, Living Christ
Wim Hof: Ice Man
Julian of Norwich: Revelations of Divine Love
Ekhart Tolle: The Power of Now

ABOUT THE AUTHOR

R.G. Shore is a Spiritual Counselor, Reiki practitioner, and energy healer, in the Pacific Northwest. He is also the founder of Northwest Wisdom, a nonprofit center for Embodied Spirituality and Healing. He is a person of color, and a formerly incarcerated person. He studies law and helps those who have been incarcerated learn to sit with their own wounds. He is specifically interested in helping people who have racial trauma and spiritual trauma.
He lives in Oregon with his wife, Jess.

Interested in learning more?

Take the companion masterclass here:

Healing Trauma Through Visual Meditation

For more information on Shore's nonprofit please visit:
www.northwestwisdom.org

Follow the author on Instagram:
@northwest_wisdom

Printed in Great Britain
by Amazon